CULTURES OF THE WORLD®

KYRGYZSTAN

David C. King

MARSHALL CAVENDISH BENCHMARK

NEW YORK

PICTURE CREDITS

Cover: © Frans Lanting/Corbis

AFP: 118 • alt.TYPE/Reuters: 26, 29, 32, 33, 36, 50, 60, 63, 78, 82, 110 • Audrius Tomonis/www.banknotes.com: 135 • Bes Stock: 1, 9, 11, 14, 15, 17, 24, 25, 67, 68, 93, 99, 117, 125 • The Bridgeman Art Library: 18, 19, 20, 22 • Camera Press: 6, 42, 43, 71, 124 • Eye Ubiquitous/Hutchison: 55, 57, 69, 75, 79, 94, 114 • Getty Images: 8, 23, 27, 31, 38, 48, 52, 53, 66, 70, 72, 74, 80, 85, 87, 101, 107, 127 • Hansrossel.com: 84 • Erik Herron: 105, 131 • Chris Herwig/PHOENIX: 42, 91, 115, 126 • Lonely Planet Images: 5, 7, 12, 39, 44, 45, 51, 56, 81, 106, 108, 109, 111, 123 • Marriage Agency of Kyrgyzstan/www.svetlanabrides.com: 3, 10, 73, 104 • Marshall Cavendish International (Asia): 129 • Panos Pictures: 13, 28, 35, 37, 40, 47, 54, 62, 64, 86, 122, 128 • RIA-Novosti Photo Library: 100 • Sergey Pyshnenko/www.karakol.kg: 4, 34, 41, 83, 95, 102, 120, 121 • Still Pictures: 30, 46, 61, 92, 96, 97, 98, 112, 113, 116, 119 • Superstock/Hubertus Kanus: 16 • TopFoto: 77 • Travel Images: 49 • TrekEarth/Azat Israiltov: 65, 103, 130 • www.avgustin.net: 58, 59, 76, 88, 89

PRECEDING PAGE

Kyrgyz mothers and their children on a dirt road in the Fergana Valley.

Marshall Cavendish Benchmark
99 White Plains Road
Tarrytown, NY 10591
Website: www.marshallcavendish.us

Series concept and design by Times Editions
An imprint of Marshall Cavendish International (Asia) Private Limited
A member of Times Publishing Limited

Library of Congress Cataloging-in-Publication Data
King, David C.
   Kyrgyzstan / by David C. King.—1st ed.
      p. cm.—(Cultures of the world)
   Includes bibliographical references and index.
   ISBN 0-7614-2013-4
   1. Kyrgyzstan—Juvenile literature. I. Title. II. Series.
   DK913.K56 2005
   958.43—dc22   2005001314

Printed in China

7 6 5 4 3 2 1

CONTENTS

These children make their own fun while playing in the Kyrgyz countryside.

A vendor sells soap, condiments, and other daily necessities at an open-air bazaar in Karakol. Also offered are a wide variety of regional dishes and fruits harvested from the area.

INTRODUCTION

KYRGYZSTAN IS A SMALL COUNTRY in central Asia, a land of snowcapped mountains, windswept desert, and grass-covered steppes. Most of the republic's 5 million people now live in settled communities, but for more than 2,000 years their ancestors were nomads, moving their herds of horses, sheep, and camels in a constant search for new sources of food.

Historically, Kyrgyzstan served as a launching pad for the armies of nomadic warriors, such as the Huns and the "Golden Hordes" of Genghis Khan, in their campaigns of conquest. Kyrgyzstan was also an outpost along the Silk Road, a caravan route that made possible the historic transfer of goods, ideas, and technologies between East and West.

Today, after 70 years of dominance by the Soviet Union, the Kyrgyz people face the uncertainty of independence and self-rule. Living in a country that has been witness to so much history helps the nation's residents face these difficulties with hope and confidence.

GEOGRAPHY

ON A MAP OR A GLOBE, Kyrgyzstan seems almost lost in the colossal mountain ranges of central Asia. Tucked within the folds of these various mountains, this former Soviet republic covers an area of 76,641 square miles (198,500 square km). Three other former republics of the Soviet Union border Kyrgyzstan: Kazakhstan to the north; Uzbekistan to the west; and Tajikistan to the south. China is Kyrgyzstan's neighbor to the east.

Two mountain ranges, the Tian Shan (Mountains of Heaven) and the Pamir-Alai, dominate the country, covering more than half of the land area and giving Kyrgyzstan an average altitude of 9,020 feet (2,751 m), or nearly 1.5 miles (2.4 km) above sea level. Lake Issyk-Kul, one of the world's largest mountain lakes, nestles in a basin 1 mile (1.6 km) above sea level. The country is landlocked; it has no coastline and does not come into direct contact with the sea.

Kyrgyzstan's location, in the heart of the great Eurasian landmass, gives it a continental climate, characterized by short hot summers and long cold winters. Because of the mountainous terrain, there are wide fluctuations in temperature and weather conditions, even within the same region. A valley area, for example, might average 60°F (15°C) in July, while higher up a mountain slope, the average could be 45°F (7°C). Still higher, a mountain pass might dip below freezing at night, even in July. Although the mountain peaks are often shrouded in clouds, Kyrgyzstan is a surprisingly sunny country. There are an average of 247 sunny days each year.

Above: **Mountaineers gather at the base camp at Khan Tengri, south of the Inylchek Glacier.**

Opposite: **Valleys such as this one are a common sight in the country's mountainous terrain.**

7

THE MOUNTAINS AND STEPPES

The mountains of Kyrgyzstan and its bordering nations are known to geologists as the Pamir Knot—the hub from which different ranges radiate like the spokes of a wheel. These mountains were created millions of years ago when the shifting of the planet's tectonic plates caused the Indian subcontinent to collide with the Asian landmass.

The force of this collision pushed the land up into some of the world's mightiest mountain ranges, including the Himalaya, Hindu Kush, and Tian Shan mountains. The process that created the towering peaks began some 100 million years ago and has not stopped since. The Tian Shan Mountains continue to grow, gaining altitude at the rate of a few inches per year.

The Ala-Archa Canyon in the Tian Shan range.

The Tian Shan Mountains, with their network of intervening valleys and basins, stretch about 1,500 miles (2,415 km) in an east-west direction, spanning a width of 220 to 300 miles (354 to 483 km). The highest peaks are in the middle of the range. Pobeda Peak (also known as Jengish Chokusu) is the tallest, reaching a height of 24,400 feet (39,284 m).

The meltwater from glaciers feeds most of the region's rivers and many of the country's 1,923 lakes, including Issyk-Kul (Warm Lake). The Inylchek Glacier, one of the world's largest, is located in an area of gigantic glaciers called Muztag (Ice Mountain) by the Kyrgyzs. Every summer enough ice melts to form Lake Merzbacher, a large lake surrounded by ice. By August, after more melting, the lake's ice banks fracture and crumble, showering icebergs into the Inylchek River below.

Different mountain elevations produce many kinds of soil and vegetation. Diverse species of animals also make their homes in the varied

A deep pool forms in the Inylchek Glacier, melted by the summer heat. The glacier's average height is 492 feet (150 m).

The Konorchok red clay canyons were formed about 1.5 to 2 million years ago. The jagged surface of the canyon is the result of thousands of years of erosion by wind and water.

habitats found at different altitudes. The most common landscape is the steppe. Similar to the prairie grasslands of North America, the steppe is a virtually unbroken prairie that stretches from Hungary and Poland in eastern Europe across central Asia to China.

For more than 2,000 years the steppes were home to nomadic tribes. Some, on horseback, formed powerful armies, using the speed and mobility of their cavalries to conquer vast areas. The great Mongol emperor Genghis Khan amassed one of history's most powerful empires in this way.

REGIONS

Kyrgyzstan can be divided into four main geographic regions. Lake Issyk-Kul and the central Tian Shan Mountains cover most of eastern Kyrgyzstan. The lake is at the bottom of a large depression, or basin, about 150 miles (242 km) long and 45 miles (72 km) wide. This is a warm, dry area. July temperatures along the lakeshore average 62°F (17°C). In January, the average temperature is 28°F (-2°C), while along the southern edge of the basin, average readings range from 90 to 13°F (32 to -10°C).

The lake itself is 113 miles (182 km) long and 38 miles (61 km) wide. Famous for the fact that it never freezes, it is just as well known for its sky-blue color and high mineral content. In fact the water is so full of minerals that it is unsafe for human consumption, although people sometimes water cattle with it.

The Suusamyr Valley is one of the major features marking the nation's second geographic region—central Kyrgyzstan. The area is made up of a high steppe plateau bordered to the north and south by vast high-elevation snowfields, with deep rivers slicing through its center. Harsh winters and the rugged terrain make this a poor farming region, best used for grazing sheep and horses. During the Soviet era, when farms operated as large collectives, as many as 4 million sheep grazed the valley. In today's harder economic climate, that number has fallen to fewer than 1 million. Instead, many families are trying to grow hardy vegetables such as potatoes and cabbages. In addition, the cool air and beautiful scenery of the high pastures in summer are drawing more and more tourists. Families offer "homestays," providing lodging for visitors who are attracted to the idea of sleeping in a yurt (a domed tent) instead of in a resort lodge.

A shepherd tends his flock on horseback near Karakol. Sheep are important to the nomadic lifestyle and diet. The traditional way of honoring a guest at a meal is to slaughter a sheep and set aside the head for the visitor.

A distant view of the Fergana Valley from the Tor Ashuu Pass shows a lush carpet of green that stretches to the horizon.

Lake Song Kul, a remote mountain lake, forms one end of this central region. The area has become popular with herders, who can take advantage of the lush pastures and a lake filled with fish.

The nation's third geographic region is the Fergana Valley, a sprawling area of grassland that stretches into Uzbekistan, where most of the valley is located. About one out of every five Kyrgyzs live in Fergana. With about 500 people per square mile, the area is the most densely populated in the country. (The average population density for all of Kyrgyzstan is 69 people per square mile.)

The valley forms a lush green oasis walled in by a different mountain range on each side. For nearly 2,000 years a main artery of the Silk Road passed through the Fergana. Before that, the kingdom of Fergana was famed for its "heavenly" horses—swift, elegant creatures believed to be the ancestors of today's Arabian horses.

During the years of Soviet rule, from about 1920 to 1991, the communist leaders in Moscow were determined to remake central Asia. This goal was part of a massive plan to have each part of the Soviet Union contribute specific products or resources to the welfare of the entire empire. The scheme was devised in order to reduce overproduction and waste.

The Moscow planners slated the Fergana Valley to become a major area for cotton production. To do this, grazing land was plowed under and rivers were dammed to provide suitable irrigation. Chemical fertilizers and pesticides were used liberally to increase production.

Workers in the valley were soon harvesting thousands of tons of cotton every year, but the experiment was ultimately harmful to both the economy and the environment. When the Soviet Union began to collapse in 1990, the market for Kyrgyz cotton collapsed with it, leading to widespread unemployment and poverty. The Kyrgyz government and people are still searching for solutions.

Western Kyrgyzstan, the nation's fourth main geographic region, is dominated by the Chatkal Mountains, an area of deep gorges, rugged cliffs, lakes, and rock-strewn valleys. Many rocks in the area feature petroglyphs (carvings and drawings on stone) dating back to the seventh century B.C. This region is home to a surprising variety of plant and animal life. Two nature preserves and a series of national parks protect several rare and endangered species.

Western Kyrgyzstan was the site of an historical battle in the eighth century when Arab armies turned back a powerful Chinese force. The victory resulted in Islam becoming the established and dominant religion in central Asia.

A worker picks cotton on a farm at the outskirts of Osh. Cotton production is still one of the mainstays of the Kyrgyz economy.

13

Cherry blossoms mark the return of spring, when parts of the Kyrgyz countryside erupt with flowers and new growth.

CLIMATE

Kyrgyzstan's location in the middle of the Asian continent, combined with its many mountain ranges, often results in extreme climatic conditions. The nation's weather can range from fiercely cold to extremely hot. The first snows of winter close the mountain passes by November, and the bitter cold continues through February. Freezing temperatures at night can continue into May or even longer at higher elevations.

Spring birds appear in March, April, or May, again depending on the altitude. From late June through mid-August, afternoon temperatures reach 90°F (32°C) or higher, although mountain valleys tend to be cooler. Like the temperature, precipitation varies considerably in different parts of the mountain ranges. In general, most of the rainfall comes in spring and early summer.

FLORA AND FAUNA

Despite its small size, Kyrgyzstan is home to a wealth of plant and animal life. Almost 1 percent of all known species are found in this country that occupies approximately 0.1 percent of the planet's landmass.

The many mountain ranges provide a variety of habitats. Forests of walnut and pistachio trees, as well as varieties of almond, apple, pear, cherry, and pomegranate trees, blanket the lower slopes in the south. The northern mountains are covered with forests of juniper and Tian Shan pine trees.

The amazing diversity in plant life includes an estimated 400 species found only in Kyrgyzstan. In spring and summer, there is a colorful procession of wildflowers, including many kinds of tulips and other bulb plants such as anemones, crocuses, and colchicums.

Animal life is also widely varied. The open steppe lands support antelope, roe deer, ground squirrels, and European red squirrels. Mountain regions are home to ibex, various kinds of marmots, and rare Marco Polo sheep with their unusual curved horns. Big cats, including tigers and cheetahs, are no longer found in Kyrgyzstan, but a rare snow leopard, or ounce, is sometimes seen. The forested mountain slopes provide the ideal habitat for wild boars, brown bears, lynxes, wolves, and foxes.

Bird life is just as abundant, with more than 360 species making their homes in Kyrgyzstan, including European birds as well as species common to China and other parts of Asia. There is a wide variety of raptors, including imperial eagles; the rare black vulture; and the lammergeier, an eagle-like vulture with a wingspan of nearly 10 feet (3 m). The wetlands provide habitat for many kinds of wild fowl as well.

Ridged and back-curving horns are a distinctive feature of the ibex. Native to Eurasia and North Africa, it feeds on a wide range of vegetation.

HISTORY

HISTORIANS CANNOT READILY identify a history of Kyrgyzstan that is separate from those of the surrounding areas of central Asia. The boundaries of Kyrgyzstan that we see on maps today are largely divisions created by the Soviet Union to serve the political needs of its dictator, Joseph Stalin. The history of this newly minted nation is the story of a region that has seen its share of turmoil and change.

In terms of the earliest human life in the region, archaeological evidence indicates that people first arrived in central Asia about 30,000 years ago. Some of the most exciting finds apply primarily to the area of present-day Kyrgyzstan: the discovery of thousands of petroglyphs created by Bronze Age peoples, beginning about 5,000 years ago. More than 10,000 petroglyphs were found strewn around a place called Saymaly-Tash (Embroidered Stones) on the slopes of Mount Suleiman. The drawings and carvings, often made with considerable skill, depict animals as well as scenes of hunting, farming, and ritual dancing.

Above: **The entrance to Mount Suleiman, where it is believed the prophet Suleiman is buried.**

Opposite: **Petroglyphs and stone sculptures such as these bear witness to the presence of the region's early inhabitants.**

NOMADIC EMPIRES

The first identifiable societies in central Asia were warlike clans known as the Scythians (or Sakas). They first arrived in the region in the ninth and eighth centuries B.C. The Scythians lived in semi-settled communities, combining farming and herding. But they were best known as warriors, a highly mobile army whose swift horses helped them overwhelm

A Chinese traveler described the Turks in the seventh century: "The khan [chieftain or leader] dwelt in a vast tent ornamented with flowers of gold, so bright they dazzled the eyes.... The remainder of his forces were made up of cavalry... dressed in furs or fine wool and bearing long lances and tall bows. So vast was their multitude they stretched far out of sight."

—Ella Maillart,
Turkestan Solo

established towns and farm villages. The Scythians built the first of a series of empires ruled by nomadic warriors that was to last more than a thousand years.

Beginning in the second century B.C., the Scythians maintained peace in the region that was threaded by the caravan routes collectively known as the Silk Road. Around the first century, the Scythians were gradually forced eastward by Persian armies and slowly faded from history. Around the fourth century, another group of nomadic clans—the Huns—swept across the steppes and mountains of central Asia reaching as far west as the Volga River. Under their determined leader, Attila, the Huns pushed onward into Rome, having a hand in the eventual downfall of the Roman empire.

In A.D. 560 the Huns were beaten by the Turks at Talas and, like the Scythians, they soon disappeared as a unified, organized society. Various

clans of nomadic Turks maintained control over most of central Asia in the sixth and seventh centuries. They established peaceful relations with the Sogdians—people of Persian ancestry who were farmers and Silk Road traders. The Turks were the first group in central Asia to leave written records and the first to mention tribes called the Kyrgyzs, who were then living in Iberia.

From about 650 to 750, the Turks and their Sogdian allies managed to hold back the powerful armies of the Arab Muslims from the west. Ultimately, they joined forces with the Arabs to beat a large Chinese army advancing from the east. In 751, at the Talas River in Kyrgyzstan, the Turks, Sogdians, and Arabs defeated the Chinese. The event proved significant because it ended the growing Chinese influence in the region. Islamic law and culture would dominate the area from then on.

Over the next three to four centuries, the Kyrgyz people gradually moved into present-day Kyrgyzstan, pressed by the relentless advance of another society of nomadic clans—the Mongols. In their new home in central Asia, the Kyrgyzs became known as shrewd traders and as

Above: **An illustration from the 13th century shows the camp of Genghis Khan. Makeshift tents housed some of the highly disciplined and well-trained soldiers who fought loyally for their leader.**

Opposite: **Scythian women fend off invaders in this illustration from the 13th century. Scythians were early settlers in present-day Kyrgyzstan. They were fearsome warriors who resisted even the attacks of Alexander the Great in the third century B.C.**

tough warriors, combining skill in horsemanship with great stamina.

THE MONGOL EMPIRE

In the early 13th century, the world witnessed the rise of one of history's most feared empires. The Mongol epoch began when a tribal leader named Temujin, who became better known as Genghis Khan, managed to unite the Mongol clans into the most efficient army of mounted warriors the world had ever seen. Genghis Khan used brilliant battlefield tactics and may have been the first to use military maneuvers and war games to train his warriors and refine his strategy.

Genghis Khan began his conquest of central Asia in 1219 and soon gained control of every oasis city along the Silk Road. He was merciless in his treatment of any peoples who offered resistance. Much of central Asia was inhabited by fiercely independent groups, mostly nomads who tried to resist the khan's domination. Hundreds of thousands died at the hands of the "Golden hordes."

The Kyrgyzs made up one of the groups that tried to fight the Mongols, but they were soon overwhelmed and nearly wiped out. Most then joined forces with Genghis Khan's armies, working as mercenaries, fighting for pay.

Genghis Khan and his hordes were known for their ruthless nature and their vicious, violent assaults. He destroyed cities, burning buildings and butchering thousands of innocent people in the process. But he gradually came to see the importance of towns and, late in his life, allowed trade to flourish again.

A portrait of Genghis Khan, whose name means "Universal Ruler." He changed his name from Temujin to Genghis Khan at the age of 42.

Genghis Khan's empire, based in China, eventually spread across Asia reaching the Caspian Sea. After his death in 1227, his sons continued to expand the empire, but the Mongol armies were unable to establish a foothold in Europe. In the late 1200s the famous Italian traveler Marco Polo crossed Asia on the Silk Road and spent several years in the Chinese court of Kublai Khan, Genghis Khan's grandson. Polo's account of the fabulous wealth of China and Japan made the people of Europe curious about these mysterious and previously unheard-of places. The hope of finding a sea route to these lands was one of the main forces driving Europe's age of exploration.

In the late 1300s another conqueror tried to emulate Genghis Khan's notorious career of war and plunder. This tyrant was named Timur and became known to history as Timur the Lame, or Tamerlane. In a nine-year period, he laid waste most of present-day Iran, Iraq, Syria, Turkey, and northern India. Tamerlane and his grandson built a fabulous capital at Samarqand in Uzbekistan, making it a major city along the Silk Road as well as a center of learning.

Shown here on horseback, Tamerlane (1336–1405) established an empire extending from Russia to India. His actual name is Timur, meaning "iron" in Turkic.

THE ARRIVAL OF THE RUSSIANS

Following the breakup of Tamerlane's empire, central Asia entered a period of disorder and economic decline that stretched into the 16th and 17th centuries. The last of the nomadic rulers controlled three separate kingdoms, or khanates. Europeans had opened sea routes to Asia, causing a sharp decline in the traffic on the Silk Road.

In the 18th and early 19th centuries, the people who would eventually be known as the Kyrgyzs found themselves cornered in their mountain strongholds, pressured by the Kokand khanate. When Russian armies began moving into central Asia, the Kyrgyzs turned to them for help. In the mid-1860s, Russian and Kyrgyz troops defeated the Kokand forces. Tashkent fell under Russian control, then Samarqand and Kyrgyzstan.

The government of czarist Russia thought of Kyrgyzstan as a colony that could provide land and opportunity for Russians, as well as for several thousand Ukrainians and Germans. The Kyrgyzs watched the Russians make many improvements, but these benefited the newcomers, not the region's native residents. Russians were also allowed to take "unoccupied" lands, but most of those lands had been used seasonally by Kyrgyz herders for grazing.

The Kyrgyzs tolerated the increasingly intrusive and heavy-handed Russian rule until 1916, when they launched a revolt that was ruthlessly put down by the Russians. Out of about 750,000 Kyrgyzs, 120,000 were killed and another 120,000 fled to China. Following the Communist Revolution of 1917–18 that transformed Russia into the Soviet Union, the lands of the defeated Kyrgyzs were made part of the Turkistan Autonomous Soviet Socialist Republic (ASSR). Not until 1936 did Kyrgyzstan become a full Soviet Socialist Republic (SSR) called Soviet Kirghizia.

Opposite: **A painting of the Russian army descending into a battle in the Russian-Turkish War, which lasted more than half a century.**

Below: **A statue of Soviet founder Vladimir Lenin stands in Ala-Too Square in the Kyrgyz capital of Bishkek.**

UNDER SOVIET RULE

Nomadic Kyrgyzs suffered heavily under the rule of the Soviets, especially when dictator Joseph Stalin launched his land reforms. Starting in the 1920s, groups of nomads were forced to live in settled communities. Then, between 1928 and 1932, thousands were compelled to live on large farms called collectives. To the Kyrgyzs, the idea of giving up their grazing lands and their herds struck at the very heart of their nomadic way of life. Many responded by slaughtering millions of horses, camels, and sheep; thousands fled to China. Opposition to this new lifestyle was cruelly suppressed, and by 1932 the collective farms had been firmly established.

In the late 1930s Stalin launched another campaign—to purge the Soviet Union of all those suspected of being nationalists (retaining loyalty to their home region) or capitalists. Several hundred Kyrgyzs, including members of the intelligentsia (the social and intellectual elite) and some *akyns*, traditional songwriter-performers, were rounded up and sent to prison camps in Siberia. Some Kyrgyz citizens were shot by the secret police.

During World War II, thousands of Kyrgyzs died fighting in the Soviet armies against the German invaders. Scholars believe that half of

the troops from central Asia defected to the German side. When Germans advanced deep into Soviet territory, entire factories were moved—along with their complete staffs of workers—to the safety of Kyrgyzstan. This boosted the country's industrial base, but also placed the country largely under Russian control.

After World War II, the growing fears of the Cold War led the Soviets to almost completely seal Kyrgyzstan's borders so that new naval weapons could be tested in secret. Uranium was also secretly mined in the region. These activities have since been suspended, and the new government is tackling the environmental damage that occurred as a result.

INDEPENDENT KYRGYZSTAN

As the Soviet Union began to weaken in the 1980s, Kyrgyzstan remained the least politically organized of the Soviet central Asian republics. Party politics were largely based on clan and regional loyalties.

Above: **The World War II Memorial, in Victory Square in Bishkek, commemorates the defeat of Nazi Germany. Today locals bring flowers to the site to pay their respects, while newly-weds use the serene and elegant surroundings as a backdrop for wedding photographs.**

Opposite: **A Soviet propaganda poster from the early 1900s.**

A Kyrgyz woman at a village polling station on election day.

Trouble developed over land and housing rights, rather than over political independence. A large area of land with an Uzbek majority had been attached to the Kyrgyz territory by the Stalinist government. In 1990 the Uzbeks, convinced that their land was being claimed for Kyrgyz housing, turned to violence. The ethnic conflict resulted in acts of brutality on both sides and claimed several hundred lives.

The Uzbek-Kyrgyz violence led many to blame the communist party leadership, and some felt the party should be disbanded. A compromise was struck by electing Askar Akaev president of the country's Supreme Soviet (the highest level of government) in October 1990. Forty-six-year-old Akaev was a respected physicist and the president of the Academy of Sciences. On August 31, 1991, the Kyrgyz Supreme Soviet voted for the declaration of independence, making Kyrgyzstan the first central Asian republic to do so. A few weeks later, Akaev was re-elected as he ran unopposed in the full presidential elections.

During the first 10 years of independence, Kyrgyzstan faced severe economic difficulties. Between 1990 and 1997, industrial production dropped by 64 percent. Current Kyrgyz leaders are also having trouble creating a sense of national unity. The mountains tend to isolate different parts of the country, and rural areas seem to have little in common with industrialized centers. To foster a sense of national unity, the year 2003 was celebrated as the 2,200th anniversary of Kyrgyz statehood, citing Chinese chronicles that showed a Kyrgyz state existed since the third century B.C.

THE SILK ROAD: CROSSROADS OF THE EAST AND THE WEST

In 138 B.C., when the Chinese general Chang Chien traveled west to the Fergana Valley in search of the powerful horses he had heard so much about, he did not realize he was founding one of history's legendary trade routes. The newly blazed trade path promised enormous possibilities. It linked East to West, connecting and opening up once-distant realms and speeding the exchange of their various goods, ideas, technologies, and religious beliefs.

With two great realms—China and Europe—at the opposite ends of the Silk Road, Kyrgyzstan occupied a key position in the middle of the great commercial route. Along inhospitable mountain trails and across harsh plateaus, caravans would wind their way to the West, bringing silks, paper, jade, furs, rhubarb, porcelain, and printing blocks. The traders going east brought ostriches, wine, linen, ivory, wool, cucumbers, and gold and other precious metals.

The caravans also carried far more valuable cargo than mere goods: the ideas, arts, religions, and technologies that were spread enriched both cultures. The East gained exposure to Christianity, Judaism, and the art and music of Europe. China received Nestorian Christianity (a branch of the faith that broke off from Byzantine Christianity in the 430s) and Buddhism (from India) via the Silk Road. Meanwhile, merchants were responsible for spreading Islam throughout the mountainous regions. The West learned about printing and paper money.

Although the Silk Road waxed and waned as a route for transporting goods and ideas, it revived in the 13th and 14th centuries with the travels of Marco Polo. The illustration (*above*) shows Venetian merchant Marco Polo (1254–1324) traveling along the Silk Road with camels laden with goods. Sea routes eventually proved more efficient, but the land route still exists today in parts. Segments have been paved, and there is talk of constructing a trans-Asian highway. Meanwhile, the National Historical Museum in Bishkek contains such relics as a third-century scrap of silk, Chinese coins, Indian cowrie-shell bracelets, iron swords, bronze lamps and amulets, and stone Nestorian crosses—all of which attest to the international nature of the route.

GOVERNMENT

WHEN KYRGYZSTAN GAINED its independence in 1991, the country found itself mostly unprepared for both democracy and self-rule. For the previous 70 years, the nation had been controlled by the Soviet Union. The Soviets insisted that Kyrgyzstan had autonomy (independence), and the constitution seemed to guarantee that. In practice, however, every major decision was made in Moscow, the capital of the Soviet empire. This dominance extended beyond political matters to include the economy and the social and cultural life of the nation. The Kyrgyz Supreme Soviet, the highest governmental body in the republic, served little more than a ceremonial function.

Above: **The first session of the new Kyrgyz parliament in Bishkek in March 2005.**

Another obstacle to establishing a working government was the lack of national unity. The nation's two major population centers—one in the north, the other in the south—were cut off from each other by mountains. In addition, people often felt greater loyalty to their family, clan, and region than to the rule of a national Kyrgyz government.

In spite of these stumbling blocks, the Kyrgyzs set to work creating an independent and democratic government. However the transition from the longtime dependence on Moscow to self-rule is a constant struggle.

GOVERNMENT AND POLITICS

The constitution created in the early 1990s provides for a democratic rule. Although Kyrgyzstan is predominantly Muslim, the government is secular, and the constitution guarantees freedom of religion as well as freedom of expression and of the press.

Opposite: **The changing of the guard at Ala-Too Square. Aside from the statue of Lenin, the square also showcases several monuments and is the location of major public events and celebrations. In the background is the State Historical Museum, previously called the Lenin Museum.**

In practice, a good deal of power is exercised by the president. One reason for this has been the charismatic leadership of Askar Akaev, the republic's first president. He was elected without opposition in 1991 and managed to win three five-year terms in all, in spite of the constitution's two-term limit. Akaev was forced from office in March 2005 during the Tulip Revolution, where Kyrgyz citizens called for the end of corruption and authoritarian rule.

The president appoints a prime minister, a cabinet of ministers, and governors for the capital and each of the seven administrative provinces, or *oblasts*. Each oblast is divided into *rayons* (districts), which are further divided and run by city, town, and village councils. The nation's parliament

Former Kyrgyz president Askar Akaev *(right)* attends the opening of the Russian air base in Kant. Walking beside him is Russian president Vladimir Putin, who joined in the ceremony held in October 2003. The air base is said to be a sign of strengthening ties between Russia and its former republic.

(Jogorku Kenesh) is made up of two chambers: the Legislative Assembly and the Assembly of National Representatives. Every five years voters elect a president and members of parliament.

In the day-to-day operations of the government, it is difficult to tell how widespread the practice of democracy is. Observers have wondered how much independence the *oblasts* and towns have had, particularly when the powerful Akaev was president. His maneuvering around the two-term limit raised questions about how fair and open the elections have been in recent years.

Akaev, however, supported a proposal to grant greater self-rule at the grass-roots level. The plan, begun in 2001, allowed voters to elect their own representative (*akim*), instead of having that official appointed by the president. The goal was to encourage people to vote and have a greater say in who will guide and improve their daily lives. So far, people have continued to vote for traditional clan leaders, but the hope remains that, with practice, people will make better-informed choices when it comes to electing their officials.

Kyrgyzstan's newly elected president Kurmanbek Bakiyev *(right)* and Kazakh president Nursultan Nazarbayev *(left)* watch a performance after Bakiyev's presidential inauguration in Bishkek. Bakiyev took office in August 2005, pledging to stamp out corruption.

KYRGYZSTAN AND WORLD AFFAIRS

Despite its remote location, Kyrgyzstan, like the other nations of central Asia, is deeply involved in major world issues. First, like many other countries, Kyrgyzstan has been affected by terrorism in this century. While terrorist cells do not seem to be operating in the republic itself, Muslim extremists have struck from neighboring Uzbekistan and Tajikistan. In 1999 four Japanese geologists working in Kyrgyzstan were kidnapped and later released by members of the militant Islamic Movement of Uzbekistan (IMU). In 2000 four American climbers were kidnapped and then also released.

The terrorist attacks on the United States on September 11, 2001, sounded a worldwide alert. It was no accident that, within four months of the terrorist assaults, the United States received permission to establish an air base in Kyrgyzstan.

The establishment of a Russian air base a few miles away revealed how important the nation was geographically. The United States used its air base, and others, to launch a bombing campaign in Afghanistan, which seemed to bring at least a temporary end to the activities of the IMU. Authorities believe that most of the organization's top leaders were killed in the raids.

Another reason for Kyrgyzstan's importance on an international level is the illegal drug trade. Afghanistan was not only a base for Islamic terrorist operations, but it is also the world's leading producer of heroin and opium—key products in the funding of terrorist activities. A large percentage of those drugs are now smuggled east across central Asia, often following routes of the old Silk Road.

POLITICS AND NATURAL RESOURCES

Kyrgyzstan is also important for its natural resources. While other central Asian countries have large reserves of oil that major powers are eager to develop, Kyrgyzstan's most valuable resource is water. Although landlocked, the mountainous country's glaciers, snowfields, and rivers make up one of the world's great sources of freshwater. The republic's neighbors already rely heavily on Kyrgyzstan's water for irrigation and depend on its hydroelectric power stations. Many Kyrgyzs feel the government has to strengthen its bargaining position in order to gain concessions, such as oil, in exchange for water.

The 12 leaders of the Commonwealth of Independent States (CIS). Kyrgyz president Kurmanbek Bakiyev is fourth from the left.

ECONOMY

FOR MOST OF THE 20TH CENTURY, Kyrgyzstan functioned much like a colony serving the Soviet Union. Kyrgyz farms and mines provided agricultural products and raw materials that were shipped to other parts of the Soviet Union. The country was totally dependent on Moscow for planning, trade, investment, and technology. Most of the consumer products people used were purchased from the Soviet Union, including items made from Kyrgyz raw materials.

When the republic gained independence in 1991, the Kyrgyz people and government began developing both a democracy and a free-market (capitalist) economy. Major economic and social measures were passed in order to shift from a communist-planned economy to a free-market system that relied on the forces of demand and supply.

THE TRANSITION STRUGGLE

During the 1990s the Kyrgyzs lived through tremendous economic upheaval. Subsidies supplied by Moscow, which had provided 53 percent of the national budget, disappeared. By 1995 agricultural output fell by 84 percent, and industrial production dropped 64 percent. Inflation soared, hitting the incredible figure of 1,300 percent in 1993, before falling to 300 percent the following year.

By the mid-1990s people's hopes surged as the new economy began to show healthy improvement, with industrial output up 35 percent and

Above: **A worker operates a smelting machine in the processing plant at the Kumtor gold mine.**

Opposite: **Farmworkers cover crops with large tarps to protect their fields from the unpredictable, sometimes harsh weather.**

agricultural production up more than 10 percent. Foreign investors showed interest, including a Canadian company that formed a partnership to open the Kumtor gold mine.

In 1998 the bubble of prosperity burst when Kyrgyzstan's three major trade partners—Russia, Uzbekistan, and Kazakhstan—faced severe financial crises of their own. The result was a sharp decline in Kyrgyzstan's growth. By 2002 Kyrgyzstan's gross domestic product (GDP) had reached only 66 percent of what it had been before independence.

Another problem that emerged during the transition years was a major loss of talented and qualified personnel, as foreign workers decided to go back to their home countries. As many as 250 left every day—primarily Russians and Germans, who took their skills and knowledge of technology and various scientific fields with them. There is no quick way for the country to fill this gap in technical expertise.

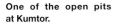

One of the open pits at Kumtor.

AGRICULTURE

Farming and herding have been especially hard hit by the transition to a free-market system. With the dawning of independence, Kyrgyzstan moved rapidly to break up the collective farms into individual holdings. By 1992, 165 state farms had been reorganized into 17,000 agricultural enterprises. And by 1998 more than half the land was owned by individuals or small cooperatives. The state, however, still controls some of the larger, more profitable collective farms, including a huge one at Kara-Balta.

The rapid move to private ownership caused a great deal of confusion. Farm families and herders often did not know how to manage operations on their own, or how to market their products, especially in the face of competition from the remaining collectives, which could afford to sell the same goods at lower prices.

Potato harvests are sometimes hampered by weather conditions, especially in the Naryn region. If winter arrives early, fuel prices rise and entire harvests are often lost when farmers cannot afford gasoline for the tractors and equipment needed to harvest the crop.

Farmers gather hay near Lake Issyk-Kul. Most hay fields in Kyrgyzstan are owned by the state, although members of the collectives established under Russian rule are entitled to farm there.

Livestock declined sharply during those hard years. The number of sheep and goats herded in the country dropped from 8.7 million in 1992 to 3.8 million in 1998. Much of the decline resulted from the slaughtering of many of the animals for food during times of severe shortage.

By the early years of the new century, agriculture was growing again. The pace of growth has been slow but steady, aided by new government measures to provide price supports and lower taxes. The major exports continue to be wool, meat, and cotton.

Even in the best of times, agriculture is severely limited in Kyrgyzstan. About 60 percent of the land can be farmed, but nearly all of that is useful only for hay fields and grazing; only 7 percent of the land is actually used for growing crops.

Despite these limitations and the hardships people have endured since 1991, Kyrgyz families have mostly grown to embrace the practice of capitalist farming. They have found that, after fertile seasons and productive years, the rewards are far greater than under the Soviet system. Even when times are hard, few long for the security of collectives, preferring instead to have their economic freedom.

INDUSTRY AND MINING

During the Soviet period (1920–91), Moscow introduced the manufacture of high-technology electronic parts. The plants relied on supplies from other republics and skilled technicians from Russia and Germany. Some factories producing mostly household products were also set up.

When the Soviet Union crumbled, so did Kyrgyzstan's fledgling industry. The market for Kyrgyz goods collapsed, factories closed their doors, and the nation lost its pool of skilled foreign workers.

Disused machinery from the Soviet era stands abandoned along a deserted road. Farm collectives and specialized industries introduced by the Russians all but disappeared in the wake of the Soviet Union's collapse. Today Kyrgyzstan leads the rest of the former Soviet republics in introducing economic reform, by moving away from a centrally planned economy to a free-market economy.

Some mining and manufacturing operations continue, but growth has been slow. The nation's most lucrative venture has been the Kyrgyz-Canadian joint partnership in the Kumtor gold mine. Opened in 1997, the valuable holding now accounts for 18 percent of the republic's GDP.

The possibility of mining other substances—including antimony, mercury, and uranium oxide—exists. But any new operations would require foreign investment, and so far foreign countries have been reluctant to become involved. Business owners say that because the federal government in Bishkek requires the filing of more than 50 forms, it is hard to get a new venture started. They also argue that a corrupt bureaucracy and system of operation gets in the way, requiring so many bribes that companies eventually abandon any development plans.

The exterior of the gold-processing plant in Kumtor. The plant produced 4.4 million ounces (0.13 million kg) of gold between 1997 and 2003.

NEW OPPORTUNITIES

Perhaps the greatest hope for the future lies in regional cooperation. President Akaev took the initiative in December 2001 by establishing the Central Asian Cooperation Organization with the presidents of three other central Asian republics: Uzbekistan, Kazakhstan, and Tajikistan. Delays happened due to the fear of terrorism in the wake of terrorist attacks in the United States in 2001, but at least the doors have been officially opened to future cooperative ventures.

The World Bank is also introducing manufacturing projects, including mining and food processing. There is also the hope that international agencies can help promote tourism. Kyrgyzstan is one of the pioneers of a new concept called community-based tourism (CBT). This plan offers tourists the chance to stay with Kyrgyz families and even to travel on horseback

Since local communities are paid directly and do not have to share profits with an agent, community-based tourism allows individuals to earn more income. Guests are also assured a more authentic experience since they stay with Kyrgyz families during their visit.

Kyrgyz cotton workers surrounded by newly-picked, snow-white cotton. With expert instruction from foreign agricultural experts, Kyrgyzstan is now exploring organic cotton production, which does not use chemical pesticides or fertilizers.

or in four-wheel-drive vehicles through mountain and highland regions. Travelers eat with the locals, following their traditional diet, and sleep in yurts—the famous portable homes of the nomads. So far, this unique form of tourism has proved successful. It provides income for local families and offers tourists an exciting new way to experience the country.

THE BALANCE SHEET

The radical change from Soviet control to independence involved both gains and losses. The Kyrgyzs exchanged the security of the Soviet system for the uncertain path of economic independence. Wages remain low, roughly the equivalent of $55 per month. United Nations agencies estimate that 63 percent of the people have incomes below the poverty line.

The Soviet system also provided free education, and there were abundant opportunities in various state-sponsored organizations such as the powerful Soviet sports machine. But the regime was repressive, and many Kyrgyzs resisted the high degree of control exerted over their lives. They also disliked being forced to give up their nomadic existence.

In the balance, most Kyrgyzs prefer the present uncertainties to what they have left behind, and they are finding new ways to make the free-market economy work for them. Some are finding ways to sell handicrafts and agricultural products at local and regional bazaars. Others have become "shop tourists," flying to Delhi, India, or Istanbul, Turkey, to buy various goods that they then resell at Kyrgyz markets and bazaars.

SHYRDAKS: SYMBOLS OF KYRGYZ CULTURE

Shyrdaks are brightly colored, appliquéd felt carpets that can be seen across Kyrgyzstan. They are portable and light and have stylized portrayals of animals or plants sewn onto them. These bold felt carpets are still found in almost every home, just as they were thousands of years ago.

Shyrdaks are made by sewing together panels of felt, each with a stylized motif or image on it. Braid is then added to the outer edges. Traditionally, two colors were used, but the availability of artificial dyes since the 1960s has provided a broader array of bold, bright hues.

Groups of women typically work together to make the *shyrdaks*. The process involves several stages. First, the wool is cleaned by spreading it over wire mesh. Two women beat it for an entire day. Then the layers of dyed or natural wool are spread on reed mats, and boiling water is poured over them. The mat is rolled up and tied with ropes, then trod or stomped on for two or three hours to fuse the wool into one layer. The mat is unrolled, more boiling water is poured on it, after which it is rolled up a second time. The women then line up in a row and kneel on the roll, beating it with their arms for about half an hour. The mat is then unrolled, and the pressed wool is left to dry.

Patterns are drawn onto the wool with soap or chalk, and then cut out. These pieces are then stitched together, and a backing of felt is added. Both appliqués and background pieces are used, so nothing is wasted.

The Altyn Oimok (Golden Thimble) workshop in Bokonbaeva, on the southern side of Lake Issyk-Kul, produces some of the best *shyrdaks*. This community workshop provides employment for single women, as well as those with large families. It buys wool from local farmers—white wool is the most prized—and uses bright artificial dyes as well as natural pigments to achieve bold and lively designs.

ENVIRONMENT

THE RUGGED MOUNTAINS of Kyrgyzstan, which cover nine-tenths of the nation, give the country its stunning natural beauty. But the harsh terrain also means that many plants and animals are confined to small, often fragile habitats. A relatively minor change in temperature or precipitation can reduce a species' chance of survival and set it dangerously on the road to extinction.

In addition to natural conditions, the environment faces some serious problems caused by humans. Many of these are the result of more than 70 years of mismanagement by Soviet planners. But some difficulties have resulted simply from the increased population density in the region. Over the past 50 years, for example, Kyrgyzstan has lost about half its forests. Much of the loss has been the result of poor timber management. Damage also occurred during the hard times of the 1990s, when people cut down acres of trees for fuel.

Over the past few years, the Kyrgyz government has become increasingly committed to environmental protection. In addition, several environmental groups have been formed and work in cooperation with UN agencies. There are 22 different ecosystems in Kyrgzystan, from deserts to alpine mountains to coniferous forests. The question is: can Kyrgyzstan do enough to restore and preserve its endangered ecosystems? Strides have been made, but continued respect for the nation's environment and valuable natural resources is essential.

Above: **Low-lying forests usually consist of fruit and nut trees.**

Opposite: **The Tian Shan range has 22 different ecosystems, resulting in highly diverse plant and animal species.**

The Toktogul Reservoir is the site of one of the largest hydroelectric power stations in Kyrgyzstan. Agreements have been made between Kyrgyzstan, Uzbekistan, and Kazakhstan regarding the use of the dam's water and the energy it generates.

THE SOVIET LEGACY

During the years of communist rule in the Soviet Union, all major decisions were made in Moscow. As Soviet bureaucrats worked out their various plans to develop their holdings, protecting the environment was not a top priority. Instead, the planners thought in terms of taming the environment, forcing it to yield the resources the communist empire needed.

Just as the radical shift to full-force cotton production took its toll on the land, so did the damming of rivers in order to increase irrigation. A good example is provided by the Aral Sea, an inland sea between Uzbekistan and Kazakhstan. Changing the course of rivers that flow into the Aral Sea has been rapidly lowering their water levels, leaving fishing villages that were once onshore stranded many miles from the water. Although this environmental disaster affects Uzbekistan and Kazakhstan more directly, the tragedy provides a lesson for all of central Asia: of the 173 animal species once found around the sea, only 38 remain. The rest have moved away or died out.

The overgrazing of pastureland was another legacy of the Soviet years. Between 1941 and 1991 there was a determined effort to increase Kyrgyzstan's livestock. While sheep and goat populations increased in all the Soviet republics, the numbers quadrupled in Kyrgyzstan to 10 million animals. Although the numbers have since been reduced to more manageable flock sizes, the overgrazing that resulted from such massive herds produced serious erosion. Today the total pastureland in the country has been reduced by one-third, and an estimated 70 percent of the remaining grassland still suffers from the effects of erosion.

The needs of the Soviet military also added to the environmental damage. The testing of top-secret weapons was conducted, especially during the Cold War years of the 1950s and 1960s, and large-scale mining for uranium in the Tian Shan Mountains was continued into the 1980s. Kyrgyzs jokingly referred to these operations as "the atomic fortress of the Tian Shan." As many as 50 abandoned mine sites may now still be leaking radioactive substances or contaminating groundwater.

Although herded animals contribute to the agricultural output, they also threaten to deplete the country's grasslands.

TODAY'S ISSUES

After Kyrgyzstan achieved independence in 1991, its government tried to address the environmental damage and impact of the Soviet years, but without much success. Officials found that the uranium mines had left behind 45 dumping sites containing an estimated 145 million tons (147 million metric tons) of radioactive and toxic waste. Some of the sites are near villages. Investigators also found that 50 business establishments were using highly toxic substances with few protected storage areas.

Cleanup efforts have been slowed by the lack of funds and technical skill. In addition, the government has not produced much legislation to

Two Kyrgyz boys walk with their cattle past a uranium waste site in the Fergana Valley. Radioactive waste was dumped into a river in the area by the Soviets.

regulate and control the activities of private businesses. For example, there were no safety regulations for trucks carrying cyanide to the Kumtor gold mine. Several accidents have resulted in cyanide being spilled into streams that flow directly into Lake Issyk-Kul.

Efforts to repair environmental damage often encounter special problems. Several reforestation and replanting programs have been launched, for example, with the goal of replacing the trees lost over the past few decades. But the harsh climate has made the task nearly impossible, even when plant species that can survive the harsh conditions have been used. Of all the trees planted since 1997, only 10 percent have endured.

Parts of southern Kyrgyzstan have higher rates of deforestation, which can result in problems such as floods and landslides.

ENDANGERED SPECIES

In 1985 a Kyrgyz Red Book was published, addressing the topic of endangered species. The report stated that 15 percent of the country's mammals and 10 percent of its bird species were threatened with extinction.

The situation is worse now. For example, tigers and cheetahs once roamed the lower mountain slopes, but they have shifted their range mostly to China. The last of a species called the Turan tiger was killed in 1972.

Mountain geese were once common throughout central Asia. They built their nests on the shores of Kyrgyzstan's mountain lakes. Environmentalists believe that there are now fewer than 30 nesting pairs in the world.

The snow leopard, the last of the big cats to make its home in Kyrgyzstan, is still seen in the higher mountain elevations, but its numbers have diminished rapidly. It is believed that about 1,000 may still be in Kyrgyzstan, with about 7,000 existing worldwide. Because the value of a single snow leopard's skin is many times that of the minimum annual wage, poaching this endangered animal is hard to resist.

One of the most common modes of transportation along the Silk Road was the Bactrian camel (the two-hump species), and many roamed wild. These camels have disappeared from Kyrgyzstan, although about 1,000 are currently found in Afghanistan.

Overhunting and poaching are placing other species in danger. Poaching is hard to stop, especially in difficult economic times, because it is one way for rural villagers to earn money. Nonetheless the impact can be devastating on some species. The saiga antelope is killed for its horns, for example, which are sold to Chinese medicine makers. Similarly, musk deer are killed for their musk glands, used in perfumes. It takes 160 deer to produce about 2 pounds (0.9 kg) of musk, so it is no surprise that the musk deer population has declined by nearly half in the past 20 years.

Opposite: **This snow leopard was rescued from poachers in Bishkek.**

Below: **The two-humped Bactrian camel was domesticated thousands of years ago. Traders on the Silk Road used these camels—as well as horses—to make their way back and forth along the famed trade routes.**

HOPEFUL SIGNS

The environmental problems facing Kyrgyzstan are severe, but recent actions by the government and environmental agencies offer considerable hope. Cooperation with UN agencies and with other central Asian countries is one particularly promising sign. There are now more than 20 nature preserves and protected areas and at least nine new national parks.

Some protected areas, such as the Sary-Chelek Biosphere Reserve, are operated in collaboration with a development agency of the European Union and with the United Nations. Sary-Chelek, covering the entire southern side of the Chatkal mountain range, provides habitats for more than one-third of the country's plant and animal species. Poaching has been a serious problem, because people living in the region have cut

Kyrgyz villagers in Andarak make their way to an event to celebrate a water project sponsored by the United Nations Development Program (UNDP). Located in the southern mountains of Kyrgyzstan, Andarak is near the border with Tajikistan. The United Nations has several ongoing projects in the area to address problems such as poverty and lack of clean drinking water.

down trees and harvested nuts, berries, other fruits, and honey, especially during the 1990s when the economy was gripped by a depression. To reduce poaching, preserve authorities are now offering alternatives, such as grants to establish tourist-related businesses.

Near Sary-Chelek is the Besh Aral Biosphere Reserve. Like Sary-Chelek, this is a region of exceptional natural beauty as well as a home to many rare plant and animal species. Besh Aral, operated in collaboration with other central Asian countries as well as with the United Nations and the European Union, includes parts of Uzbekistan and Kazakhstan. The preserve staff provides education, training, and financial aid for local populations, while also overseeing the use of pastures and forests.

One of the most ambitious projects in central Asia is the in-development Issyk-Kul Biosphere Reserve, which will link several existing preserves as well as add to them. The plan includes controlled land use for farming and herding, as well as community-based tourism. When completed, the preserve will be nearly as large as Switzerland.

The placid waters of the lake stretches to the horizon in the Issyk-Kul Biosphere Reserve.

KYRGYZS

THE TOTAL POPULATION of central Asia is about 60 million people, and few areas of the world have experienced such a blending of peoples. More than 80 national and ethnic groups are scattered throughout the region. The ebb and flow of peoples across the continent for more than 20 centuries have added to the melting pot that is modern-day Kyrgyzstan. In addition, the Soviet system of drawing national boundaries has left groups of one nationality residing inside another country, such as the Uzbeks who now live within the borders of Kyrgyzstan.

About two-thirds of the population is Kyrgyz, with an estimated 23 national and 60 ethnic groups making up the other 33 percent. The exact figures have been difficult to determine since independence, because thousands of Russians and other national minorities continue to return to their homelands.

THE KYRGYZS

The people who are currently known as the Kyrgyzs are one of the oldest ethnic groups recorded in Asia, first mentioned in the second century B.C. Typically a fair-skinned people with green eyes and reddish hair, they began as a loose confederation of tribes, moving south into central Asia from Siberia, starting in the ninth century. Some migrated to present-day Kyrgyzstan to get away from wars, and thousands came as soldiers in the Mongol armies of Genghis Khan.

Above: **A Kyrgyz girl in traditional dress.**

Opposite: **Skateboarders and inline skaters gather in Ala-Too Square.**

A poster showing some of the peoples of Kyrgyzstan. A 1999 census revealed that the country consists mostly of Kyrgyzs, Uzbeks, and Russians. It was the first-ever national census, and in order for it to be as accurate as possible, the government attracted the people's interest by including a lottery where valuable prizes were given away.

By the time these migrations ended in the 1500s, the Kyrgyzs had formed a solid majority in the area that became Kyrgyzstan. They lived primarily as herders, raising Asian fat-tailed sheep, goats, Bactrian camels, and, above all, their tough Kyrgyz horses. The horses became a great source of individual wealth. They provided meat and *koumiss*, a favorite drink made of fermented mare's milk. The horses and camels were also used in the Kyrgyzs' role as transporters working along the Silk Road.

A Kyrgyz's identity and place in society depend in large part on his or her tribal and regional origins. The Kyrgyzs are divided into roughly 30 tribes, or *sanjiras*, and the tribes are clustered into two regional groups. The groups are quite distinct, and they are in constant competition for political power and influence. One group consists of the northerners, or Tagai, who also include Kyrgyzs who are living in Kazakhstan. The southerners, or Ich Kilik, include Kyrgyzs living in Tajikistan and China.

The northern tribes include the Sary Bagysh, which is the tribe of the former president Akaev and those closest to him. These northern tribes have lived with Russian settlers for several generations and tend to be more Russified than Kyrgyzs who settled in other parts of the country. The southern tribes, through greater contact with Uzbeks, have adopted a more devout approach to Islam. The northern and southern groups have also developed some language differences to the extent that they can sometimes have difficulty communicating.

These tribal and regional networks continue to be important. Although the government hopes to reduce the influence of the tribes, they continue to provide the path to political appointments. Connections gained through them can also be critical in getting a job or promotion, even in obtaining a better booth for one's wares at a bazaar.

Bazaars are vital for the purchase of food and daily necessities as well as the exchange of livestock. They attract large crowds everywhere. Connections and personal influence within a tribe can help a vendor secure better locations in which to realize a tidy profit.

A Russian girl in a music store. Most Russians in Kyrgyzstan live in Bishkek or in the Chui Valley area.

DWINDLING MINORITIES

The breakup of the Soviet Union led to confusing shifts in population throughout Europe and Asia beginning in 1990–91. Many Russians left Kyrgyzstan to return to their native country in order to take part in the rebuilding of their newly independent homeland. The same was true of other national minorities: Ukrainians, Georgians, and East Germans.

Later in the decade, ethnic tension and conflict caused more migrations. Russians in particular felt that they were being pushed out by being denied opportunities for jobs and government appointments, even though there had been many Russians in the country for 150 years. Between 1989 and 1999, an estimated 273,000 Russians left Kyrgyzstan, reducing the Russian population by one-third.

The same feeling of exclusion led many Germans to leave, reducing their numbers by 61,000, which represented nearly 80 percent of that minority. Similarly, a seemingly small number of Ukrainians left—36,000, or roughly half of their original population in Kyrgyzstan.

OTHER MINORITIES

Uzbeks are the largest minority group in Kyrgyzstan, representing about 14 percent of the population. Most live in and around the Fergana Valley, which is a natural geographical extension of Uzbekistan. Uzbeks have traditionally supported themselves through farming and trading. Their lifestyle and their deep devotion to Islam set them apart from their Kyrgyz neighbors.

The boundary area between Uzbekistan and Kyrgyzstan has erupted in violence several times since independence. In addition to the ethnic fighting of the early 1990s, in 1999 and 2000 the extremist Islamic

An Uzbek woman selling fabric at the Osh bazaar.

Above: **Children who fled to Kyrgyzstan after violence broke out in their villages in Uzbekistan. About half of the population in Osh is Uzbek, although they do not have any formal political representation.**

Opposite: **Two women display their traditional dress, complete with unique headdresses.**

Movement of Uzbekistan (IMU) launched a series of raids across the border, occupying towns and taking hostages. After Kyrgyz troops drove the renegades out, the Uzbek government decided to plant land mines along the border between the two countries. It is believed that key IMU leaders were killed when the United States invaded Afghanistan in 2002, prompting the IMU to stop its aggressive actions.

The Uighurs are a smaller group, making up only about 1 percent of the population. They are related to the Uzbeks and are also farmers and traders. Most Uighurs live near cities such as Bishkek and Osh.

Several other central Asian ethnic groups are represented in the country's population. Tatars, Kazakhs, Tajiks, and Turks combined make up only about 2 percent of the population, but they add rich variety to Kyrgyz life.

Villages around Bishkek, and in the capital city itself, are home to two small but growing groups, Dungans and Koreans. The Dungans are Chinese Muslims. The Koreans lived around Vladivostok in the Soviet Union until World War II when Joseph Stalin, fearing that they might be spies for the Japanese, had them deported.

Both groups worked hard to establish themselves. Some worked in specialized agriculture, while others entered technical professions such as electronics. Today, Dungans and Koreans are among the most prosperous people in Kyrgyzstan.

DRESS STYLES

For special occasions, both Kyrgyz and Kazakh women wear similar kinds of clothing: long dresses with stand-up collars. Or, instead of high collars, they might wear brightly colored vests and heavy jewelry. Women also favor fur-trimmed headdresses topped with crane feathers. An older woman often wears a turban—the number of times it is twisted and wound around her head indicates her status.

Men almost always wear a white felt cap called an *ak kalpak*. It is usually embroidered and has a tassel. In winter, older men wear long sheepskin coats and round hats with fur trim.

LIFESTYLE

THE KYRGYZ WAY OF LIFE is still deeply influenced by their long history as a nomadic people. Hospitality, for example, is of great importance. Any stranger is always welcome to share another's home and food. If a family lives in extreme poverty, the members will still give all they can to their guests. This kind of hospitality helped people survive in the almost lawless days of the Silk Road, when travelers had to rely on the goodwill of those they encountered.

While friendly to strangers, Kyrgyzs are often distrustful of people in authority. In their nomadic life, the people relied on their village elders and their tribal leader. If a leader became overbearing or misruled in other ways, they would either remove him from power or else pack up and move to another tribe.

In the 20th century, Soviet authorities thought this distrust was directed at communist rule, so they tried to crush anything that seemed like opposition. The Kyrgyz response was to appear to be obeying Soviet authority while secretly maintaining their own traditional lifestyle. By living this kind of dual existence, they managed to preserve a great deal of their traditional culture.

Above: **University students in Bishkek take a break in between classes.**

Opposite: **A newly-wed couple and their families after their official ceremony in Bishkek.**

LIFE IN BISHKEK

Bishkek, the capital, is by far the largest city in the republic, with a population of about 650,000 people. It is the hub of business and industry, as well as the seat of government, and it has the greatest mixture of

People having a leisurely stroll along a broad promenade in Bishkek.

ethnic and national groups. In spite of the exodus of non-Kyrgyzs, more than 40 percent of the people are Russian. The appearance of the people, and of the city itself, is more Russian than Asian. Kyrgyzs make up only about 30 percent of the population, and the remaining 30 percent is a mixture of many different backgrounds.

The broad streets, laid out in a grid pattern by Russian planners, make it easy to get around. Residential areas feature Russian- and Ukrainian-style houses, with curved eaves and gardens of apricot, apple, and shade trees. In fact Bishkek is one of the greenest cities in central Asia, with stately oak trees gracing the parks and lining the major streets.

In this kind of setting, it is not surprising that the mood of Bishkek tends to be relaxed and easygoing. Office workers lunch in a park or an open-air café when the weather permits. For men, *chaykanas* (teahouses) are favorite gathering places. While women are permitted to enter, the *chaykanas* are considered special retreats for men. They are usually located in a tree-lined area near a stream. The men sit on a bed-size platform

64

covered with a carpet and with a low table in the center. Fortified with endless cups of tea, the men can talk for hours.

While Russians and other Europeans are emigrating, more and more of the "new Kyrgyzs" are arriving, many now with sufficient training to work in businesses, government departments, or the growing number of international aid agencies.

Many less prosperous people have also crowded into the city, living in congested conditions on the edges of the city. They find that selling souvenirs, tobacco, and candy as street vendors is better than suffering through another bitterly cold winter in the countryside.

Architecturally, Bishkek is a new city. Almost none of the buildings predates World War II. The earlier settlement on the site was a post on the old Silk Road, but it was destroyed by the relentless violence of Genghis Khan's armies in the 13th century.

In Bishkek newspapers are put up on notice boards like these, so that anyone can read them.

A woman sits at the entrance of an amusement park in Bishkek.

Later, in the early 1800s, the Kokand khanate built Pishpek on the site as a fort to protect the caravan routes. In 1926, after the Soviet Union gained control, it was renamed Frunze in honor of a hero of the Russian Revolution. During the 1970s and 1980s, the Soviets' communist leadership oversaw construction of the city's most visible buildings: a series of huge marble-faced structures in the city center, called Ala-Too Square, including the National Historical Museum, the "White House" (where both the president and the parliament have their offices), and the monumental Philharmonia building.

Behind Ala-Too Square is Panfilov Park, where families gather on weekends and on mild evenings. Rides and arcades, built during the Soviet years, make this the heart of the city for kids. Another relaxing leftover from the Soviet era are public baths, such as Zhirgal Banya, which feature hot and cold baths, steam baths, and a rubdown with birch branches.

Shopping is an almost daily activity for many families, and the city's bazaars, or marketplaces, are always busy. There are three daily bazaars:

one where food is sold, another for clothing, and a third for household items. On weekends the Dordoy Bazaar is like a North American flea market, filled with people and alive with activity. It is nicknamed *Tolchok,* which means "jostling crowd."

RURAL LIFE

Roughly two-thirds of the nation's population live in rural areas; and, for many, life has been hard since independence. Under Soviet rule, most rural families lived and worked on large collectives, herding or growing cotton and food crops. Now that herders and farmers are on their own, earning a living has proved more challenging, and many families live below the poverty line. Still, most eke out a living. Many are finding ways to add to their families' income. Some lead hunting parties, for example,

A young boy rides a horse with ease and confidence. The horse is an essential part of Kyrgyz life and culture due to the long history of domestication and its importance as a symbol of prestige, a means of transportation, as well as a source of income.

and others guide hikers into mountainous areas. With community-based tourism, some families make small sums by maintaining yurts for vacationers. In addition, a growing number of women are forming cooperatives to help them market their crafts, such as carpets and other felt objects.

Much of the Kyrgyz lifestyle reflects the people's nomadic past, even if Kyrgyzs now are established in permanent communities. Some continue to live a semi-nomadic existence. For about 2,000 years, the remarkably mobile yurt formed the center of their lives. Most Kyrgyzs today prefer the comfort of modern houses, especially in winter. When summer approaches, however, many miss the outdoor living and closeness to nature offered by a yurt. Some families move into yurts for the summer in high meadows, while others construct them in their gardens.

THE LIFE CYCLE

The Kyrgyzs are fond of celebrations, and every major stage of a person's life is occasion for a feast. Not only is the birth of a child cause for a party, but there are also celebrations for a baby's naming, for the ninth day after birth, even for the first haircut.

Marriage is one of the most important social functions, because it strengthens the ties between families. Traditionally, marriages were arranged, and this practice is still followed in some rural areas. Usually the deal is struck when the boy is between 12 and 15 and the girl is a little younger.

The meal at celebrations is not much different from the daily evening meal. It begins with a prayer, followed by tea. The head of the family then breaks or cuts bread and distributes a little to everyone. This is followed by nuts or sweets as appetizers. The main meal is eaten off the serving plate, using either large spoons or hands.

GENDER ROLES

As a nomadic society, the Kyrgyzs adopted a less strict attitude toward Islam, integrating those elements that seemed to fit most comfortably they saw radically new opportunities open up for them in the areas of education and careers.

Above: **Nomadic Kyrgyz women and girls inside a yurt. Today, there are programs to promote women's political, social, and economic interests. The United Nations Development Program has also set up a Women's Bureau in Bishkek and women's resource centers in other communities.**

Opposite: **A young boy dons the traditional felt hat worn by men. One Kyrgyz practice for newborns is that they are only introduced to relatives and friends 40 days after birth. A gift of money for the child is appropriate on such an occasion.**

69

In many ways, however, the old patriarchal (or male-dominated) system never disappeared. A woman, even when married, occupies the lowest status in the household, and normally she lives with her husband's family. She is not supposed to address the males in the family by name, referring instead to "your father's youngest brother." She usually wears a headscarf in the house and is expected to serve guests.

The most extreme illustration of the lingering male-dominated system is bride kidnapping. While the practice is now illegal and diminishing in Kyrgyzstan, there are several cases each year of false kidnappings in which a man runs off with a woman he wants to marry. He takes her to

About half of the agricultural workforce in Kyrgyzstan consists of women.

Dilde Sarbagysheva, the Kyrgyz ambassador to the United Kingdom, presents her Letter of Credence to the British monarch Queen Elizabeth II at the Buckingham Palace in 2005.

his parents' home, then sends a message to her family requesting their permission. The family almost always agrees, since it would bring shame on them to refuse. Usually the kidnapped bride knows her abductor, and sometimes the couple plans it together as a romantic adventure. There are still instances, however, of actual bride kidnappings in which the man's identity is not known, and the woman's family tries everything in their power to get her back.

In spite of such traditions, most Kyrgyz women generally enjoy fewer restrictions on their lives than women in other central Asian countries. They go to college, run businesses, and are also increasingly active in politics. In 2002 one-third of the country's elected officials were women, although they rarely attained positions in the higher levels of government.

These small towers are mausoleums where the deceased are laid to rest. A traditional funeral can stretch for 40 days, where a feast is provided. In cities, families sometimes rent restaurants for this purpose. However the costs of such funerals can drain a family's finances, and Muslim leaders are now advising people to refrain from such lavish ceremonies.

FUNERALS

The Kyrgyzs show a remarkable respect for the dead. A funeral is a large and expensive affair including an elaborate gravestone that is decorated with tiles and often features a dome or turret. The funeral ceremony lasts about 10 days, followed by a one-year period of mourning. Two yurts are constructed, one for female mourners, the other for the body of the deceased. The family of the deceased is expected to slaughter cattle and horses to serve visitors as they come to pay their respects.

Friends and family gather to mourn, with a great outpouring of emotion. Horse meat—the most expensive food—is served along with *pilov*, a rice-and-meat dish. After three days of mourning, the deceased is buried in a white cloth. In some tribes, a woman on a white horse reads a poem, then rides off. After that, women are excluded from the funeral.

For another seven days, men gather to read the Koran. The Kyrgyzs believe that the deceased is alone at that point and needs this special companionship. Throughout the year of mourning, people visit the family and the cemetery. Finally, a year after the burial, the gravestone is erected. This is usually the occasion to slaughter an animal for a feast. Family members continue to visit the grave on holidays, such as Remembrance Day on June 13.

EDUCATION

Kyrgyzstan's education system suffered with the breakup of the Soviet Union. Not only did the nation's schools lose funding, but many of the nation's educators were Russians who promptly left for their homeland.

Officially founded in 1997, the American University–Central Asia in Bishkek began as the Kyrgyz-American School (KAS) as part of the Kyrgyz State National University (KSNU). Today it is an American-style liberal arts university.

73

A teacher with her class. Students begin their primary education at the age of 6, attending four to five hours of lessons each day.

Schooling is still compulsory up to age 16; and it is free, although families are expected to make some contribution.

In the 1990s the literacy rate reached a peak of 97.3 percent but has since dropped slightly. More teachers and additional funding are needed. Some private institutions, such as the American University in Bishkek, have opened primary schools, but tuition is required so that only the children of wealthy families are able to attend.

Education for girls beyond the elementary grades has suffered the most. In the Soviet system, girls accounted for more than half of the high school and college students, but this number has been declining since the country achieved independence.

One of the few bright spots has been an increase in institutions of higher learning. The number of colleges and advanced training institutes has tripled since 1991. Much of the increase has been due to foreign institutions such as the Turkish University in Bishkek.

THE YURT—A SIGN OF THE NOMADIC PAST

For centuries the yurt—a portable circular dwelling of timber and felt or animal skin—has been a central part of the lives of Kyrgyzstan's nomadic peoples. *Yurt* is the Turkish word for "home," and even though today's most common dwellings are brick structures or Soviet-style apartment blocks, the yurt still retains its grip on the country's imagination. As a symbol of national identity, the yurt is even represented on the flag

(by the *tunduk*, the circular frame of wooden spokes around the smoke hole at the top). Yurts are now set up for festivals and funerals and are used in the summertime in gardens or when shepherds take their flocks high up in the mountains to graze.

The construction of a yurt has changed little over thousands of years. A framework of poplar poles (*kanats*) is bent and fixed with straps and leather nails into a domed circular tent. A trellis wall (*kerege*) is erected to keep the shape. Woven reed mats line the walls. Several thick layers of felt form the outside, and these are tied to strong poles dug into the ground. There is a smoke hole at the top, although today people use stoves with chimneys. Inside, the yurts are lined with brightly colored *shyrdaks* for warmth and comfort.

The interior is laid out in the traditional manner, with the left side reserved for men and their horses and hunting gear. The right side, for the women, contains the stove and cooking utensils. At the back, a richly carved cabinet or chest holds carpets and blankets for sleeping; these are spread out on the ground, which is covered with *shyrdaks* at night.

The portable yurt is easily assembled and carried from place to place on horseback or by wagon. In the past, the building of a new yurt was traditionally celebrated with great festivities. The words "May smoke always rise from this yurt! May the fire never go out of it" were spoken as a ram's head was tossed high into the air. The clan chief counted his subjects by the number of *tyutyuns* (columns of smoke) rising from their yurts; this word is still used today in villages to tell how many households there are.

RELIGION

THE RELIGION OF ISLAM, founded by the Prophet Muhammad in the early 600s, expanded rapidly in the seventh and eighth centuries. Spread mostly by Arab armies, it soon was practiced throughout the Mediterranean world, much of the Middle East, and then across central Asia. Initially most of the nomadic tribes of the region did not embrace the new religion. This was especially true in the reign of present-day Kyrgyzstan, where Islam only became the official religion in the 10th century, and even then the conversion was piecemeal.

As with so many elements of culture and cultural borrowing, the Kyrgyzs adopted those Islamic beliefs and practices that met their needs and discarded the rest. For example, they never fully adopted the Five Pillars of Islam, even though these are regarded as the religion's basic principles. When a mullah (religious teacher or leader) was available, he would conduct weddings, funerals, and daily prayers. If no mullah was in the village, the people proceeded on their own.

Early in the 19th century, when the khanate of Kokand gained control of the country, the khan's officials tried to oversee a more thorough conversion to Islam. This was quite successful in the southern part of Kyrgyzstan, close to the devout Muslims of Uzbekistan. North of the Tian Shan Mountains, however, people were more heavily influenced by Russian industry and culture, so that region remained more secular. To this day, these differences in religious belief still contribute to the ongoing tensions between northern and southern Kyrgyzstan.

Above: **Followers pray at the Babur's Mosque in Osh.**

Opposite: **A mosque in Naryn. About 75 percent of the Kyrgyz population are Muslims.**

Under the Five Pillars of Islam, devout Muslims are to:
1. Believe that "There is no other God than Allah [the Arab word for God], and Muhammad is his Prophet";
2. Obey the five daily calls to public prayer;
3. Fast during daylight hours throughout the holy month of Ramadan;
4. Pay a special tax to help the poor; and
5. If physically able, make at least one pilgrimage to the holy city of Mecca.

YEARS OF UPHEAVAL

Kyrgyzstan experienced years of painful and chaotic change in the 20th century. The Soviet takeover after 1917 involved a sweeping economic revolution, one which brought the Kyrgyz nomadic way of life to an abrupt end. The tribespeople were ordered to turn their herds and flocks over to the state and to move onto huge collective farms. Those who resisted were dealt with harshly; often they were banished to forced-labor camps in Siberia, or were simply executed.

Many people found that Islam offered some solace during these troubled times. They began attending prayer services in mosques and made pilgrimages to holy shrines. It was not long, however, before Soviet authorities cracked down on organized religion. Land and property

Muslim men attend a Friday prayer service.

owned by all religious groups—Christians, Jews, Buddhists, as well as Muslims—was confiscated. Religious leaders were persecuted.

From 1932 to 1936 Joseph Stalin supervised a campaign called "Movement of the Godless," his determined drive to create a religion-free state. Mosques were closed or destroyed. Mullahs were arrested as spies or enemy agents. Of the 47,000 mullahs who had served throughout central Asia in 1930, only 2,000 were still alive by 1941.

The Kyrgyz response to the repression was to move their religious observances underground. A mystical sect called the Sufis helped to keep the practices intact. During World War II, in order to boost wartime morale, Stalin eased up on his brutal campaign. But, as soon as the war ended, the campaign resumed. In addition the Soviets tried to promote atheism (having no belief in the existence of a god) as superior to any

Nomadic children reading the Koran. Traditional Kyrgyz practices are often incorporated into the practice of Islam in Kyrgyzstan.

religion. During the 1950s, for example, the Tian Shan Komsomol (the youth branch of the communist party) sponsored hundreds of lectures on topics such as "What Every Atheist Should Know."

Then, during a period in the 1960s known as the Khrushchev Thaw, Soviet premier Nikita Khrushchev had an uncharacteristic change of heart: he decided that the traditional Kyrgyz way of life was better suited to the steppe environment than collective farms growing cotton. Suddenly, rural Kyrgyzs were able to return to their beloved semi-nomadic life, moving their livestock to the high pastures for the summer months.

ISLAM TODAY

With independence, full freedom of worship has been restored, and the government has an official policy of tolerance of all religions. There has been a flurry of mosque-building throughout the country, although this is less noticeable in the north, where Islam is still not widely practiced.

The September 11, 2001, terrorist attacks on various locations in the United States sent shock waves across central Asia. In addition to allowing the United States to establish an air base near Bishkek, the Kyrgyz government has begun monitoring the activities of Islamic organizations. There has been growing concern over a group called Hizb ut-Tahrir, for example, because it favors the creation of a separate Islamic state in the Fergana Valley. Although the group opposes the use of violence, there has been some fear that extremists could seize control. Few Kyrgyzs have any interest in Islamic fundamentalism, however, and there has been no evidence of extremist activity.

A wall mosaic shows Kyrgyzs of different races and religions coming together, united under the single identity of the republic. The Kyrgyz government believes in promoting intercultural tolerance, which is taught in schools.

Parishioners attend a service in a cathedral in Bishkek.

SUFISM

Sufism has been around for hundreds of years. It was never an organized religion or movement but rather consisted of individuals who sought through deep prayer to achieve a more direct union with God. Sufis are deeply religious or mystical people. They follow a variety of "paths" to achieve a trancelike state which enables their spirits to be in contact with God.

In the early years of Islam, many Sufis acted as missionaries. They were particularly active along the Silk Road. Today Sufism is often regarded as the mystical side of Islam. Probably for this reason, Sufis are not welcome in fundamentalist Islamic states such as Iran.

OTHER RELIGIONS

The early years of the 21st century have witnessed an increased presence of various Christian organizations in Kyrgyzstan. The Seventh Day Adventists, Baptists, Jehovah's Witnesses, and others have tried to gain converts. But the great majority of Kyrgyzs have expressed little interest in changing their religion. They consider themselves to be Muslims, even if they have never entered a mosque and do not answer the daily calls to prayer. Especially during the uncertainty of the past few years, Islam continues to be a unifying force, one that has provided stability for Kyrgyz culture.

Like other elements of Kyrgyz culture, the practice of Islam includes beliefs from nomadic days that have been fused with standard Islamic ideas and practices. A holy site often includes a wishing tree, for example, a carryover from a pre-Islam belief system. Other ancient practices include consulting with non-Muslim holy men, or shamans.

About 20 percent of the Kyrgyz population belong to the Russian Orthodox Church. Most of the believers are ethnic Russians.

SHAMANISM

Shamanism may well be the world's oldest belief system, dating back to the Stone Age. Like Sufism, it is not an organized religion, but instead consists of a variety of practices based on the idea that everything on earth and in the heavens contains a spirit. Through the efforts of a shaman, this spirit world can be contacted to help humans in some way, such as healing or revealing the future.

The word *shaman* in the Tungus-Manchurian language means "one who knows." (The Kyrgyz word is *bakshi*.) Throughout history, both men and women have been shamans, and it is believed that in Kyrgyzstan today, women practitioners outnumber men.

Shamans were a basic part of tribal life during the centuries when the people of central Asia were mostly nomadic. The shaman often prophesied about such matters as when to move the herds and flocks, when to go into battle, or when to retreat. Warriors often requested that a shaman make a ritual sacrifice on the eve of battle, so as to ensure a favorable outcome.

Evidence of shamanism can be seen among the steppes and pastures, where stone figures, called *balbals*, are scattered. Near Bishkek, a group of *balbals* has been marked off as a sort of open-air museum. These date as far back as the sixth century. *Balbals* are thought to represent defeated opponents or deceased khans. Sometimes graves were excavated from below these stone figures.

Through a variety of different practices, the shaman entered a trance, enabling him or her to travel to different spirit worlds. These travels are described in Kyrgyzstan's eloquent epic poems and songs.

One of the major roles of shamanism has been in healing, and it is as healers that most shamans continue to function today. Rural Kyrgyz families are likely to seek a shaman for a medical problem while also going to a doctor. Some shamanistic practices can be even carried out without a shaman present, such as waving a smoking juniper branch around the house to ward off evil spirits.

Чын курандын тартуу.

Ж

Тема: Кезек

акылдуу

рдуулук,

рамдуум

мдуулук

гүкөрлүк

LANGUAGE

THE KYRGYZS have a remarkable respect for language. Even those who are illiterate admire someone who speaks clearly and fluently. The Kyrgyzs especially love the sounds of their homeland's traditional poems and songs.

A 19th-century Russian anthropologist described their love of language this way: "One cannot but admire how the Kyrgyz people master their language . . . . They express their thoughts exactly and understandably, making their speech somewhat graceful . . . . That is why the folk poetry of the Kyrgyz has reached such a high level."

THE TWO-LANGUAGE PROBLEM

Throughout the Soviet era, the dominant language spoken in Kyrgyzstan was Russian. People quickly learned that it was the language of the educated and that speaking it fluently was essential for advancement in government. The Kyrgyz language was tolerated, and it became the social language—used at home and on the street.

Soon after independence was achieved in 1991, the government announced that Kyrgyz would be the new state language. For some time the announcement sparked little change, and language usage remained much as it had been before. Many Kyrgyzs were startled to discover how spotty their knowledge of their own language was. At the same time, Russians and members of other minorities resisted having to learn the complicated Kyrgyz language.

So little progress was being made on the language front that the government postponed the deadline for the use of Kyrgyz in all government

Above: **Readers pick up a copy of a political periodical outside the Osh market.**

Opposite: **A student practices her writing in a Kyrgyz language school.**

A mother reads aloud to a child as a friend listens on. There are no recent data reflecting the actual rate of literacy in the country.

business until 2005. Also, in May 2000, the government decided to add Russian as a second official language on an equal footing with Kyrgyz. It was hoped that this move would persuade Russians and other Slavic groups not to emigrate.

The establishment of Kyrgyz as the state language increased the tensions between northern and southern Kyrgyzstan. Many young southern Kyrgyzs headed for Bishkek and other cities after independence, hoping to find work. They discovered that northern young people, often applying for the same jobs, tended to have an advantage because they spoke Russian and some Kyrgyz, while rural southerners spoke Kyrgyz only. Feelings ran so high that the conflict sometimes became violent.

For most people, it was strange and sad to see the country divided over what seemed to them a minor language problem. The majority do not really care how fluent their leader is in Kyrgyz. They are far more interested in the person's ability to improve their lives.

In addition, those difficulties have not prevented people from appreciating the country's rich legacy in the Russian language. As one poet expressed it, "Through the Russian language, we've had the entire world of Russian and world literature opened to us. What a wondrous legacy!"

MODERN KYRGYZ

Kyrgyz is a Turkic language that was written in the Cyrillic alphabet for much of the 20th century. The alphabet is similar to Russian Cyrillic.

 АЛТЫ ДИН КЕЛИМЕСИ
Аъуузу биллаахи минашшайтоонир-
рожиим
Бисмиллаахир рохмаанир рахиим.
1 - Лаа илааха иллаллооху
Мухаммадур росуулуллоох.
2 - Ашхаду ал лаа илааха
иллаллооху. Ва ашхаду анна
Мухаммадан ъабдухуу ва росуулух.
3 - Лаа илааха иллаллооху вахдахуу.
Лаа шарайка лахуу лахул мулку, вала-
хул хамд, йухйии ва йумииту, ва хува
хаййул ла ямууту, биядихил хойру,
ва хува ъалаа кулли шай-иҥ кодиир.
4 - Субхааналлоохи вал хамду лиллаахи.
Валаа илааха иллаллооху, валлооху
акбар, валаа хавла валаа куввата, иллаа
биллаахил, ъалиййил ъазыйм.
5 - Астагфируллооха,
астагфируллооха, астагфируллооха
таъаалаа миҥ кулли замбин, азнабтухуу
амдан, ав хатаа-ан, сирран, ав ъалаа
ятан. Согыйратан ав кабийротан ва
уубу илайхи миназзамбиллазии

1

The country is currently trying to make a transition to an exclusive use of the Roman alphabet, as are its central Asian neighbors. While the change has gone quite smoothly in Uzbekistan and Turkmenistan, the Kyrgyzs have had a harder time. The change to Arabic numerals, on the other hand, was quick, and all vehicle license plates have the internationally accepted numbers.

For those individuals who are still struggling to master Kyrgyz after years of relying on Russian, the change has not gone as smoothly. The following phrases below will demonstrate how complicated the process is.

An Islamic prayer book from Kyrgyzstan. It is written in Cryllic instead of the usual Arabic.

English	Kyrgyz	Russian
My name is . . .	*Menim auym . . .*	*Meenya zavoot . . .*
What's your name?	*Sizdin atiyngyz kim?*	*Kak vass zavoot?*
Where are you from?	*Siz kaidan kelgensiz?*	*Viy otkooda?*
I'm from . . .	*Men kelgem . . .*	*Ya eez . . .*
Any children?	*Baldariyngyz barby?*	*Dyete yeest?*
What is your job?	*Kaida ishteisez?*	*Kto viy po profyessy?*

SOME BASIC KYRGYZ WORDS AND PHRASES

Here are some Kyrgyz words in a modified Roman alphabet:

Hello.	*Assalam aleykum.*
Good-bye.	*Jaksy kalyngydzar.*
How are you?	*Kandai siz?*
Yes/No.	*Ooba/Jok.*
Do you speak English?	*Anglische suyloyalasezbe?*
bread	*nan*
meat	*et*
rice	*kuruch*
tea	*chay*

PRONOUNCING KYRGYZ CYRILLIC LETTERS

Cyrillic	Approximate Pronunciation	Cyrillic	Approximate Pronunciation
А а	"ah"	Р р	rolled "r"
Б б	"b"	С с	"s"
В в	"v" (pronounced as "f" when ending the word)	Т т	"t"
		У у	"oo," as in "boot"
Г г	"g," as in gull	Ф ф	"f"
Д д	"d" (pronounced as "t" when ending the word)	Х х	"kh," as in the Scottish "loch"
		Ц ц	"is"
Е е	"yeh"	Ч ч	"ch," as in "chin"
Ё ё	"yo," as in "yacht"	Ш ш	"sh"
Ж ж	"zh" (Kyrgyz as in "jolt," Russian as in "pleasure")	Щ щ	"sheh" as in "fresh cheese"
		Ы ы	"iy"
З з	"z"	Э э	"e," as in "egg"
И и	"ce," as in "week"	Ю ю	"yoo," as in "use"
Й й	"y," as in "yet"	Я я	"ya"
К к	"k"	Ь ь	"soft sign"—softens the preceding letter
Л л	"l"		
М м	"m"		
Н н	"n"	**Additional Letters**	
О о	"o," as in "horse" when stressed or "ah" when unstressed	θ θ	"Ó," as in "church"
		Ң ң	"ng"
П п	"p"	Y y	say "e" and round your lips

NONVERBAL COMMUNICATION

The Kyrgyzs have a variety of ways of greeting one another, and the procedures are followed in an almost ceremonial way. When two men who are friends greet each other, for example, the handshake is not overly vigorous, but it is warm and often quite elegant. Good friends can also shake hands by lightly and gently placing them, with the thumbs up, in between the other's hands. It is not unusual for men to simply touch wrists, especially when they are working and their hands might be dirty.

Women do not usually shake hands. Instead each touches the other's shoulder, using the right hand. And, as a sign of respect, a younger woman will kiss an older woman on the cheek.

The Kyrgyzs are also fond of hugging. Any festive gathering is likely to include a lot of hugs.

Women exchange kisses and warm hugs during a festive celebration.

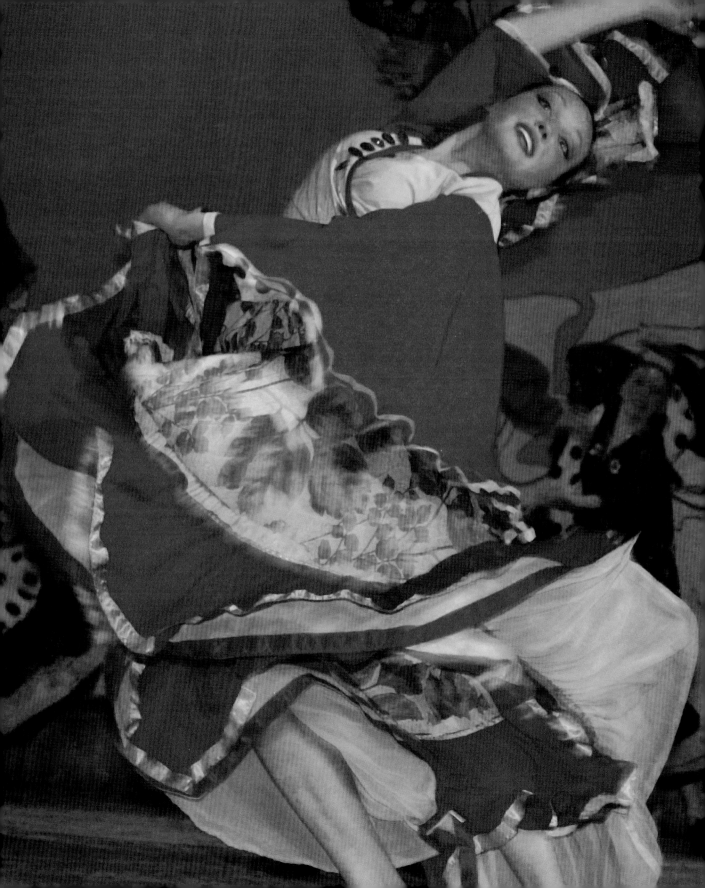

ARTS

THE ARTS OF CENTRAL ASIA reflect the long history of people who followed a nomadic way of life. Much of the region's art centers on horses, the yurt, and the steppe environment. The Kyrgyz made elaborately carved yurt doors and beautifully crafted saddles. Poems and songs were inspired by simple natural events, such as mist rising from a mountain lake or an eagle soaring across a valley.

Kyrgyz art needed to be moved easily and quickly. The *shyrdaks* that decorated the walls of the yurt and added to its insulation were folded up in minutes, like the walls of the yurt itself. Beautifully crafted jewelry was not only an art form but also a convenient way to store and transport wealth. Storing tales, poems, and songs in one's memory was far easier than transporting a library of books.

AKYNS: *TRAVELING BARDS*

Kyrgyz literature is based on a long and remarkable oral tradition. For centuries, songs, stories, and poems were sung and recited by special performers called *akyns*. Each of these traveling minstrels, or bards, relied on a memorized repertoire of lyrics and tunes. When invited to a wedding, anniversary, or other celebration, the *akyn* recited long passages and improvised new lyrics to fit the special occasion.

The Kyrgyz word *yr* refers to all the *akyns'* literary forms: poems, songs, and stories. All *yrs* carry a message—ethical, moral, or philosophical—

Above: **An** *akyn* **strums on his** *komuz*, **in accompaniment to his moving recitation.**

Opposite: **A graceful dancer twirls about in her eye-catching costume at a celebration of Independence Day.**

93

designed to offer hope, encouragement, and sometimes guidance. They were particularly important in times of heavy warfare or during a conflict with another tribe.

The most honored of the *akyns* were called the *manaschis*. They were the narrators of a vast collection of oral stories called the Manas Epic.

THE MANAS EPIC

The Manas Epic is a cycle of oral legends and songs, some 20 times longer than the Greek classic, the *Odyssey*. Like the epics of other cultures, the Manas Epic tells of the origins of the Kyrgyz people through the many heroic deeds of a legendary warrior named Manas. The cycle also includes amazing stories and heroic deeds involving his wife, Kanykei; their son, Semetei; and a grandson named Seitek.

Performers at the Manas Celebration Complex in Talas. Celebrations for the 1,000th anniversary of the Manas Epic were held in 1995.

More than 1,000 years old, this collection of heroic tales consists of the myths, stories, and legends of the Kyrgyz people which have been passed on orally from generation to generation. It is such an integral part of the national identity that in 1995 the Manas Celebration Complex in western Kyrgyzstan was built to celebrate 1,000 years of Manas and the epic named for him. The United Nations extended the honor by declaring 1995 to be the "International Year of Manas."

The hero of the epic, the great leader Manas, embodies such virtues as bravery, justice, and national pride; he is always depicted as skilled in horsemanship and the martial arts. The oral tales and songs relate his adventures as he searches for a homeland for his people. As the tales unfold, they offer moral insight and even guidance in how to deal with everyday problems.

This monument of the legendary hero Manas in Bishkek shows him on his steed named Ak Kula.

The *manaschis*, the special singers of the Manas Epic, are often trained in the profession from an early age. A child can receive a special calling when the Manas spirits come to him or her. A famous *manaschi*, Ulukhabar Atabek, said, "When I recite the epics, it leaves my heart feeling very light. You can't teach it, you either know it or you don't. It comes from God."

Although the oral tradition is mostly a thing of the past, the Manas Epic is available in contemporary forms. During the Soviet period, folklorists recorded the tales, which have been translated into the various languages and dialects of Kyrgyzstan. Since independence, the stories have been made available as novels, plays, television shows, poems, and even comic books. In a revival of the earlier days of the *akyns*, present-day bards,

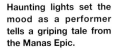
Haunting lights set the mood as a performer tells a griping tale from the Manas Epic.

often in sequin-decorated costumes, keep the stories and songs alive, but this time in crowded auditoriums instead of in yurts.

The Manas Epic will continue to thrive as part of the nation's heritage. It offers courage and hope, imbues the people with pride, and is also a unifying force as the Kyrgyzs struggle to build a viable democracy and a healthy economy. The Kyrgyzs were fortunate that the strength of their oral tradition survived the Soviet era. Under Stalin, the communists brought literacy to central Asia. They also made a concerted effort to silence if not destroy the literary traditions of the Kyrgyzs and others, fearing those traditions might feed anti-communism. But Soviet agents could not erase the influence and power of the Manas Epic and other Kyrgyz oral tales and poems.

Performers practice a violent scene from the Manas Epic on Independence Day.

A young musician performs with a *komuz* at a children's festival.

MUSIC

All *akyns* accompanied their recitation and improvisation with a variety of musical instruments. The most common of these was a three-stringed instrument called a *komuz*, or a *kyyak*, a similar instrument played with a bow and having two strings. Other musicians might join in with wood, brass, horn, or clay instruments, producing haunting sounds. Percussion instruments were used to add important background sounds such as chimes and, above all, animal hooves pounding the hard earth. With or without accompaniment, skilled *akyns* can keep their audience enthralled for as long as 24 hours.

Traditional Kyrgyz folk songs are also popular in the nation, as are song-and-dance troupes. These groups play at urban nightclubs and also at community celebrations. The guitarlike *komuz* is the basic instrument, along with drums, flutes, long horns, and mouth harps (*temir komuz*), or a mouth harp that includes a string (*jygach ooz*).

TOKTOGUL: BELOVED BARD

One of the most famous and beloved of the *akyns* was Toktogul, whose name means "Halt, slave of God!" He was born into a poor family in 1864, high in the western Tian Shan Mountains. As a boy, he performed songs while herding sheep. In his teens, he joined a traditional contest in which two singers make up derisive lines about each other. His competitor was the local noble's court singer. Toktogul won the contest with the best lines, and his competitor withdrew. It was then that Toktogul made a *komuz* for himself and became a wandering *akyn*. He played with such agility that it often sounded as if his *komuz* was speaking in different languages—Uzbek, Kyrgyz, Russian, and Kazakh. He even imitated birdcalls.

Toktogul gained a reputation for fighting oppression by performing songs critical of the nobles. This made them report him falsely to czarist authorities. He was taken from his wife and young son to a hard-labor camp in Siberia. The initial journey from the Caspian Sea to Moscow gave him the chance to share many songs. He became a favorite with his fellow prisoners, and when they brought him a *balalaika* (a Russian guitar) he sang haunting songs of loss and loneliness. On his third attempt in 1910, he managed to escape successfully, but when he returned to his beloved Tian Shan he found his son dead and his wife remarried. Of his son he wrote:

"Swans on a far-off lake
Their burning sorrow can slake.
In the steppes the gray falcon can stay
Till the wind its sorrow blows … away.
O my son, can anyone … anywhere
Relieve me of my despair?"

Despite this tragedy, Toktogul continued performing and his fame grew. Eventually, he gained a few students. When he was arrested again in 1913, his pupils were able to collect enough livestock to have him set free. The Soviets claimed Toktogul was a socialist for refusing to sing for the nobles. His eulogy for Lenin suggested his sympathy for communism by containing the words, "Even if my jaw were to fall away I would keep on singing about the happy life that has come to my people."

Toktogul died in 1933. Even though he fell into disfavor with the authorities, he continues to be a popular figure with the Kyrgyzs. There is even a town named after him; and a reservoir, a literary museum, and a street also bear his name.

LITERATURE

Kyrgyzstan does not have a strong tradition in conventional literary forms. Throughout most of the country's history, very few Kyrgyzs could read and write. That changed when the Soviets set up a modern education system. Along with literacy, however, the communists also brought an insistence on "socialist realism," the idea that the arts should depict the heroic struggle of workers and peasants against the oppressive capitalist system. The Kyrgyzs had little interest in that kind of literary theme.

The one novelist who has managed to rise above the limitations of the Soviet system has been Chinghiz Aitmatov (1928–), the only Kyrgyz writer to achieve an international reputation. Beginning in 1963 with *Tales of the Mountains and Steppes*, Aitmatov produced a dozen highly praised novels. Writing first in Kyrgyz, then in Russian, he made keen observations on the country.

In the 1980s Aitmatov dared to explore themes that had once been taboo under the Soviet regime. In *The Day Lasts Longer Than a Hundred Years* (1981) and *The Place of the Skull* (1989), he dealt with religious conflicts, environmental issues, and Kyrgyzstan's increasingly serious problem with illegal drugs.

FILMS

Early in World War II, when German armies were swarming deeper into the Soviet Union, west of the Ural Mountains, several factory towns were moved to Kyrgyzstan to keep up production in the Soviet war industries. One result of this unusual migration was the establishment of a small film studio in 1942. Russian immigrants and Kyrgyz film buffs produced a small number of highly regarded feature films, newsreels, and documentaries. The best-known film producer today is Aktan Abdykalykov. His film *Beshkempir*, or *The Adopted Son*, was selected to be screened at Cannes, France, the site of one of film's most prestigious festivals.

Opposite: **Kyrgyz author Chinghiz Aitmatov.**

Below: **Patrons outside a film theater in Bishkek.**

HANDICRAFTS

Some traditional handicrafts were lost in the late 19th and the 20th centuries under the influence of the Soviets and the pre-Soviet Russians. Kyrgyz embroidery, for instance, was replaced by Russian and Ukrainian styles and techniques.

The *shyrdaks* have undergone changes, but today seem to be returning to more traditional designs and techniques. The artificial dyes of the 1960s produced brightly colored appliqués, for example; but many women are now going back to the softer tones created by natural dyes, such as those

Opposite: **Wooden Kyrgyz dolls, with their distinctive hats, are sold as souvenirs.**

Below: **Handcrafted toy Bactrian camels, made from felt.**

made from raspberry leaves, birch roots, and pear leaves. Neutral colors, without dyes, are also gaining in popularity.

In addition to the *shyrdaks*, other handicrafts also reflect the nomadic past, when mobility was so important. *Ayak kaps*, for instance, are woven bags that are hung on yurt walls for storing plates, clothing, and other items. Embossed leather bottles are also still being made and these were used for storing and transporting *koumiss*.

Small decorative creations are also sold as souvenirs. These include dolls in Kyrgyz dress, camels, and birds made from wood or felt.

Kyrgyzstan is part of the Central Asian Crafts Support Association, which promotes the indigenous art of the region. Items such as handbags, purses, and pencil cases are also made with traditional motifs.

Kyrgyz craftspeople continue to produce outstanding jewelry, usually working in silver and semiprecious stones. In nomadic days, men carried their wealth in the form of swords and daggers that had jeweled handles and sheaths. Women's jewelry was equally elaborate and valuable. It was said that, when on the move, a wealthy woman might be wearing so much jewelry that walking was difficult. All of these items are still available in city bazaars, some as antiques, others as replicas.

LEISURE

THE PACE OF LIFE in Kyrgyzstan can be slow. In rural areas it closely follows the seasons and the movement of the herds to and from the high summer pastures (*jailoos*). People work hard, especially in the struggling post-Soviet economy, and they do not have much time for leisure.

Since the Kyrgyzs have traditionally had a strong bond with the natural world, especially as nomadic herders, it is not surprising that they often spend their leisure time engaging in outdoor activities. There are few of the indoor activities familiar to Westerners. Television and movie theaters are found only in major urban areas, for example, and activities such as board games are uncommon, except for the ancient board game of *nard*. Nor are the Kyrgyzs usually avid readers of books. However, many enjoy spending hours listening to the clever improvisation and recitations of the *akyns*.

TEA DRINKING

Kyrgyzs are fond of visiting family and friends, and this frequently involves the ceremony of drinking tea. The activity might take place in a home, in a yurt, or—in urban areas—in a *chaykana*, or teahouse.

People drink tea from a small bowl, a *piala*. The host often pours the first cup, then throws it away in order to clean the *piala*. Next, a *piala* of tea is poured out twice and returned twice to the pot to brew the tea. The *piala* for a guest is filled only partway, allowing the host to refill it

Above: **Nard** is a board game similar to backgammon.

Opposite: **Boys on horseback at a resort in Toguz-Bulak, a popular skiing spot in the southeast of Bishkek.**

A girl with a calf at a Sunday animal bazaar, where horses, donkeys, sheep, and camels often change hands.

often to keep it warm. Throughout this time-honored procedure, people talk. The combination of tea and conversation is considered a perfect way to spend an afternoon or evening.

BAZAARS

Every town has a colorful market, or bazaar; and a favorite pastime, especially on Sundays, is to spend the day there. Some are essentially farmers' markets. The stalls are piled high with fresh and dried fruits (except in winter), peanuts, walnuts, bread, eggs, meat, and honey.

Every bazaar also has a number of food stalls, each with its own specialty. The food is served with tea or *ayran*, a yogurt drink. In the continuing tough economic times, older women called *babushki*, or grandmothers, spread blankets outside the bazaar on which they arrange their items to sell: matches, pens and pencils, candies, and chewing gum.

One of the most popular bazaars is the *mal bazari*, or animal market, on the northern edge of Karakol. Hundreds of people gather for the Sunday event, some having traveled for several days. They represent the wide diversity of central Asian ethnic groups, and they come to buy and sell horses, cattle, sheep, goats, pigs, and sometimes a camel. It is a noisy, festive scene marked at times by the excitement of someone test-riding a horse by galloping through the crowd.

HUNTING, FISHING, AND GUIDING

For many Kyrgyzs, activities such as hunting and fishing are often means of providing a little extra food or income for the family. A short trip by vehicle or on horseback in any direction can lead to the spectacular scenery, and hunting grounds, that Kyrgyzstan is famous for. A small number of Kyrgyzs still employ a unique way of hunting—by using a golden eagle. In nomadic days hunting with eagles was quite common, and there are still a few hundred practitioners today. A trained eagle can bring down

A hunter is accompanied by a falcon perched on his arm. Hunting with birds is an ancient skill passed down from the Mongols. The hunter trains the falcon to obey his commands and also to identify the different kinds of animals to hunt. The falcon can kill small animals such as badgers and foxes. Sometimes they are made to work in pairs.

small game such as rabbits or foxes. Spectators enjoy the speed and skill that are displayed. Hunters sometimes use falcons too.

The lakes and streams of Kyrgyzstan are teeming with fish. A typical fisherman on a stream feeding Lake Issyk-Kul might expect to catch four or five trout every hour. Foreign visitors as well as Kyrgyzs are discovering the country's pristine lakes, like the seven famous lakes at the Sary-Chelek Biosphere Reserve.

As the number of foreign visitors has increased, more and more Kyrgyzs are earning money by acting as tour guides. Visitors from Europe and the United States come for trekking, mountaineering, and rock climbing. These visitors have discovered that Kyrgyzstan has some of the world's most spectacular scenery, and that local guides are essential to make the most of the experience. The Kyrgyzs, in turn, have the opportunity to enjoy these leisure activities while they are earning an income.

Right: **Hikers enjoy the clean mountain air and colorful scenery of a lush canyon in Ala-Archa.**

Opposite: **A young Kyrgyz rider wearing a traditional hat matched with a modern denim jacket. The horse proved central to the region's economy as well as to its recreation.**

The nation's beautiful, unspoiled mountains and valleys have proved increasingly popular. A trek can be a hike of a few hours or a backpacking adventure ranging from a few days to three or four weeks, traveling either on foot, on horseback, or in a four-wheel-drive vehicle. Mountaineering is more rigorous and involves climbing peaks or struggling through rugged mountain passes.

SPORTS ON HORSEBACK

The Kyrgyzs generally show little interest in sports that are popular in the West, such as soccer, golf, or sailing and boating. But no society in the world is more famous for its equestrian games. These sporting contests, some dating back 1,000 years or more, are fast-paced, rough, and sometimes violent. While the games are not as common as in the nomadic past, almost any modern festival is an opportunity for these wild and colorful sports.

The best-known of the equestrian sports is called *kok boru*. The game is played with a headless goat, one that has also had its lower legs and entrails removed. After being soaked in cold water overnight to toughen it up, the goat carcass is placed in a circle at one end of a large field.

Competitors participate in Kyrgyzstan's roughest sport, *kok boru*. The headless goat's carcass is tossed about on the dusty ground as participants scramble on horseback to seize control of it and score a goal.

At the other end of the field, any number of players wait, seated on their tough, wiry Kyrgyz horses. At the starter's signal, the players race across the field, competing either as individuals or as teams. One player grabs the carcass and tries to carry it down the length of the field, around a post, then back to the circle where he drops it and is declared the winner. Of course, a crowd of other riders is just as eager to stop him and take away the prize.

To spectators, the game appears to be a chaotic war on horseback. Men and horses come together in a wild, noisy struggle, until one rider will suddenly break loose dragging the carcass, with the others in pursuit. According to legend, the game originated as a military training exercise in the days of Genghis Khan to develop the kind of daring and skill that warriors needed.

Other equestrian games are also popular, both for participants and for spectators. These games are usually played in the cooler months of spring and autumn. In a game called *tyin enmei*, participants try to pick coins off the ground while riding at full gallop. *Jumby atmai* is archery on horseback; and in *oodarysh*, contestants wrestle while on horseback. *At chabysh* is a more traditional horse race, but it is run over a distance of 15 to 20 miles (24 to 32 km). All of these games involve prizes: such as money, a rifle, or a *chapan* or cloak.

In a game called *kyz kuumai* ("chasing after the bride"), a man chases a woman, both on horseback, and tries to catch her and kiss her. The woman is given a head start as well as the faster horse. If the woman successfully avoids her pursuer, she gets to chase the humiliated man and, when she catches him, give him a few whacks with her whip.

A Kyrgyz couple getting ready for their coupling ritual, *kyz kuumai.*

FESTIVALS

THE KYRGYZS RARELY PASS UP an opportunity for a celebration. The occasion might be a family event, such as a wedding or the birth of a child. Or it might be a formal festival celebrating a day of national importance such as Independence Day.

The festivals follow an ancient tradition, dating back hundreds of years. Whenever a khan was newly elected, a great festival was held that brought together tribal leaders from across central Asia. The great festival included then, as it does today, an enormous feast; games on horseback; and storytelling and songs by the *akyns*, weaving in any new tales about recent events or new leaders.

NOORUZ

Nooruz (New Day) is one of the most popular festivals in all of central Asia, also observed by many Afghans and Iranians as well as Kurds in Iraq, Turkey, and Syria. This special day features a unique array of foods. It began more than 1,000 years ago as a shamanistic celebration of the arrival of spring. The holiday became included in the practices of Islam and was originally scheduled according to the lunar calendar, which meant that the date shifted each year. Over the past century, it gradually became fixed on March 21, the spring equinox.

In the mid-20th century, Soviet authorities banned the festival, fearing that it might weaken people's loyalty to the Soviet system. In 1989 the Soviets suddenly reversed their position. Nooruz again became an official holiday, but as a secular event, with no religious overtones.

Above: **Young performers put up a show at the annual international "Young Talents" Festival, where youths from around central Asia showcase their performance arts.**

Opposite: **A girl waves a Kyrgyz flag during a Nooruz festive parade.**

113

A crowd in Bishkek celebrate Nooruz with traditional food followed by performances.

Today it is celebrated with great fanfare, including street fairs, storytelling, games on horseback, and feasting. Some of the dishes that are prepared are unique to this holiday. One traditional dish, prepared only by women, is *sumalak*. It is made with wheat that has been soaked in water for three days until it sprouts. The wheat is then ground, mixed with oil, flour, and sugar, and then cooked over low heat for 24 hours.

Another dish is *halim*, a cereal of boiled meat and wheat grains, seasoned with black pepper and cinnamon. Still another dish, which is also popular during the month of Ramadan, is *nishalda*, made from whipped egg whites, sugar, and licorice flavoring. Ramadan is the ninth month of the Islamic calendar when believers fast from sunrise to sunset for the entire month.

The table also always includes seven items, all beginning with the *sh* sound: *sharob* (wine), *shakar* (sugar), *shir* (milk), *shirinliklar* (candy or dessert), *sharbat* (sherbet), *sham* (a candle), *shona* (a flower bud, symbolizing the renewal of life).

In addition to feasting, music, dance, and the traditional equestrian games, people join hands around a burning juniper log in the hope of having a good harvest.

In 2004 Nooruz in the border regions of the Fergana Valley took on an intercultural theme as Kyrgyzs and Takjiks who lived in the area came together to celebrate. Many came in their distinctive traditional costumes. The occasion included delicious cuisines, spontaneous dances, and a friendly marathon.

A young performer at a Nooruz celebration rehearsal in Bishkek.

OFFICIAL HOLIDAYS IN KYRGYZSTAN

January 1	New Year's Day	May 9	Victory Day (World War II)
January 7	Russian Orthodox Christmas	May 29	Armed Forces Day
January 14	Old New Year's Day (Pre-Soviet)	June 13	Remembrance Day
February 23	Men's Day (formerly Soviet Armed Forces Day)	August 31	Independence Day
March 8	International Women's Day	September 1	First Bell Day (First Day of School)
March 21	Nooruz (Islamic Spring Festival)	First Sunday in October	Teachers' Day
May 1	Labor Day		
May 5	Constitution Day	November 7	October Revolution Day

FAMILY CELEBRATIONS

Family celebrations, or those involving just the local community, generally follow the same pattern as the great national festivals. The building of a new yurt, for example, includes the usual feast, the telling of witty stories, dancing, and then special rituals. A typical ceremony involves tossing the head of a ram into the air while shouting the words: "May smoke always rise from this yurt! May the fire never go out in it!" In the past, even breaking camp when the tribe moved on involved a special custom. Everything was done according to a set pattern, accompanied by special songs.

Other celebrations vary, depending on the occasion. Certain rituals and foods are associated with different events in a child's life. Jentek Toi, for example, is a family festival celebrating the birth of a child; Kyrkan Chygaruu celebrates the 40th day after the birth; and Tushoo-Kyrkuu is the party for the first birthday. Another group of celebrations is for a wedding, including the announcement of the nuptials, the actual event itself, and the bride's first visit to her parents' home after the wedding.

Sometimes a new yurt is built for a newly married couple. The outer embroidery is sometimes simple but the colors are always bright and attractive.

Special meals are prepared for national festivals and for local celebrations. A bright white tablecloth is placed on a low, round table. The meal starts with a prayer and tea. Different kinds of bread are placed on the table, along with fruits and sweets. A variety of appetizers is served, along with *koumiss*, the country's favorite beverage, made from fermented mare's milk. Some of the dishes may not suit the tastes of Westerners. A favorite appetizer, for example, is *choochook*—a sausage made of specially prepared horse fat.

The main part of the meal is likely to include *beshbarmak*, a dish made of horse-meat sausage, broad noodles, and a sauce. Another favorite is *samsa*, a pastry filled with meat, onions, and the fat of a lamb's tail.

A Kyrgyz woman getting ready to prepare a festive spread in the cooking area of a yurt.

A performance during the nationwide celebration of Independence Day.

(Kyrgyz sheep are a breed known for their large, fatty tails.) *Samsa* is cooked in a special clay oven called a *tandyr* and is served straight from it. The meal is also accompanied by more *koumiss* or *ayran*. More tea or, on special occasions, several rounds of vodka conclude the meal.

THE MANAS FESTIVAL

The Manas festival celebrates the legendary life and heroic acts of Manas. As with other festive events, the Manas celebration involves songs, storytelling, horseback games, and a feast.

The festival is held on or near Independence Day, August 31. In 1995, when the event celebrated "1,000 years of Manas," President Akaev used the occasion to promote national unity. In a speech, he identified the "seven principles of Manas": patriotism, national unity, humanism, cooperation among nations, hard work, education, and strengthening the Kyrgyz state system. Since 1995 the Manas festival has been tied closely to Independence Day and the virtues of freedom.

FOOD

KYRGYZ FOOD IS SIMILAR to that of the Middle East in its reliance on rice, savory seasonings, vegetables, yogurt, and grilled meats. Some popular dishes are borrowed from other countries, including *pilov*, also known as rice pilaf; and nan, a flat bread found throughout Asia.

Some of the foods were part of the nomads' basic diet, consisting mostly of meat, milk products, and bread. As people adopted a settled lifestyle, they developed, or borrowed, dishes such as pilafs, kebabs, noodles, and stews, plus fancy breads and pastries.

Seasonings are usually mild although some sauces can be extremely spicy. The most common spices are black cumin, red and black pepper, barberries, coriander, and sesame seeds. Common herbs include dill, parsley, celeriac (the root of a kind of celery), and basil. Wine vinegar and fermented milk products are also standard.

POPULAR DISHES

Lamb is the most common meat. The fat-tailed Kyrgyz sheep are prized for their meat as well as their wool. Fat from the sheep's tail is esteemed more highly than the meat itself. One of the most common ways to serve it is *shashlik* (lamb kebabs). Kebabs are also made of beef, chicken, or other chopped meats.

Pilov is so commonplace that some travelers have assumed it was the only thing the Kyrgyzs could cook. *Pilov* consists of rice with boiled or fried meat, onions, carrots, and raisins or fruit slices. This is a common dish served to guests.

Above: **An array of spices used in cooking dishes from various cultures is available at the nation's food bazaars, which are busiest on Sundays.**

Opposite: **Pieces of nan stacked for sale at an open-air food bazaar.**

121

Central Asian noodles, or *laghman*, are different from noodles found elsewhere. *Laghman* is often used as the base for a spicy soup—also called *laghman*—and includes fried lamb, peppers, tomatoes, and onions.

Two other popular soups are *shorpa*, made with boiled lamb, tomatoes, carrots, and turnips; and *manpar*, which consists of noodle bits, meat, and vegetables in a broth with mild seasoning. Salads are not a common, everyday food. In response to the requests of travelers, though, a *salat tourist* is served consisting of sliced tomatoes and cucumbers. Other salad items, such as parsley, fresh coriander, green onions, and dill, are served and eaten whole.

Nan, the flat bread that is served at every meal, is baked in tandoori ovens. This simple staple is sold in most places, and a traditional home meal is never complete without it. Some varieties are prepared with onions, meat, sesame seeds, or the fat from the tail of a sheep.

Right: **The delicious laghman is believed to have originated from western China.**

Opposite: **A woman milks a mare. Mares produce milk when they give birth to foals, which is during spring and summer.**

SNACKS

Various meat-and-dough snacks are sold by street vendors. Some are steamed meat dumplings; other varieties are boiled, baked, or fried. These can be served plain or with sour cream, butter, or vinegar. Another common street food is *piroshki*, a Russian fried pie stuffed with meat or potatoes.

Fruits are also popular. They are eaten fresh, cooked, dried, or made into jams, preserves, and a drink called *sokh*. Other favorite snack items include all kinds of nuts and dried fruits: walnuts, peanuts, and almonds mixed with raisins and dried apricots.

DAIRY PRODUCTS

The Kyrgyzs are fond of fermented dairy products, especially mare's milk, which has an alcohol content of about 4.5 percent. The milk of cows, sheep, goats, and camels is also used.

Soured milk is used to make yogurt. The yogurt can be strained to make *suzma*, a tart cream cheese used as garnish or added to soups.

Another milk product is *kurtob*, which is dried *suzma*, shaped into small, marble-size balls. Kyrgyzs carry these when they travel, since it is a nutritious snack that never spoils.

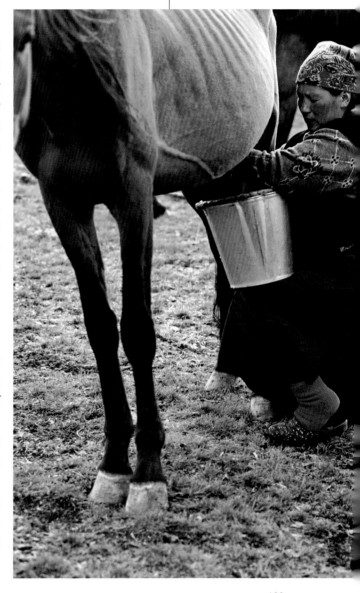

BEVERAGES

Koumiss is the best-known Kyrgyz drink, but the fermented mare's milk has a strong taste that many people find offensive. Tea is a more common mealtime drink. A runny yogurt called *ayran* is also popular, as is *maksym*, a thick drink made from wheat which is sold at street stalls during the summer.

Except for *koumiss,* alcoholic drinks were virtually unknown until the Russians arrived. Russian vodka, which the Kyrgyzs call *arak*, has had an unfortunate impact on Kyrgyz society. Especially during hard economic times, drunkenness and alcoholism have become problems. German-made beers and a yeasty Russian drink called *kvas* are also available in restaurants.

A woman serves an elderly man *koumiss.*

DINING OUT

In the years since independence, there has been a rapid increase in the number of urban restaurants, catering to the new class of city office workers, professionals, and foreign travelers and businesspeople. These establishments offer a wide variety of foods, from central Asian to Chinese, Turkish, Korean, Russian, and a range of European cuisines as well.

Kyrgyzs prefer eating at home, but when they do eat out it is likely to be at one of the local canteens. Canteens are cafeterias—and usually look much like school cafeterias. The best canteens are generally found in government buildings or at universities. The food has the reputation of being hearty and inexpensive.

There are practically no conventional restaurants in small cities and towns. Instead, a few families operate home-style eateries. There are usually no signs indicating the existence of a restaurant. Instead, the owners literally invite people on the street to come in.

Men enjoying tea and one another's company at an open-air teahouse.

Seated around the spread that is placed on a cloth on the floor, everyone has their legs tucked in, ensuring that their feet do not point at anyone.

DINING CUSTOMS

No matter how poor a Kyrgyz family is, the main meal follows common practices. In Muslim families, for example, the left hand is considered unclean, so it is not used for handling food at the table. People receive dishes with their right hands and use only their right hands for raising food to their mouths.

A *dastarkhan* is a large cloth spread on the floor that serves as a dining table. People seated around a *dastarkhan* are careful not to step on it. When seated around the cloth, it is also customary not to let your foot point at any other diner.

Bread is regarded as a sacred food. Everyone at a meal is careful not to throw it away or place it on the ground. Whenever bread is offered, it is polite to break off a piece and eat it.

The *amin* is a prayer of thanks that ends the meal. No one eats after the *amin*. The prayer often consists of moving cupped hands over the face as if washing. Women as well as men commonly use this gesture.

HOSPITALITY

In Islamic cultures a guest holds a position of honor, whether the person is Muslim or not. Hosts will extend every act of hospitality to a guest, even if they have very little food for themselves. If you are invited to a Kyrgyz home for a meal, there are several standard customs that guests are expected to follow.

A family welcomes a guest with a generous spread of local delights.

First, you should arrive with a gift. This can be something simple, such as a basket of fruit or something for the children. The most favored gift would be items from your home, such as postcards or photos. You should definitely not offer to help pay for the meal.

When you enter the house, remove your shoes. A pair of slippers or flip-flops will be provided. If you are offered water for washing your hands, do not refuse. And it is thought to be rude to shake the water off your hands. Do not sit down until your host directs you to a spot—usually opposite the door so you will not be disturbed by others bringing and clearing dishes. It is also believed that this seat is the warmest in a yurt. Men, and women from another country, might dine separately from the women and children of the host family.

After a prayer, tea, bread, and appetizers, the main dish is likely to be *beshbarmak,* a feast of large flat noodles with horse meat, usually in the form of sausage, cooked in a vegetable broth. The name means "five fingers" because it was traditionally eaten with the hands (right ones, of course) or with large spoons.

Other festive dishes, including *pilov,* are also included; and bread is always present. If you eat too slowly, people will ask if something is wrong. If you eat too fast, your plate will instantly be filled again.

A village community celebrates with a feast. There is no sequence of courses to a Kyrgyz meal, as in most Asian cuisines. The dishes, including fruits, are served all at once.

Kyrgyz hospitality can cause the guest embarrassment in several ways. One awkward moment might occur if the host has slaughtered a sheep for the occasion, which happens usually to mark a special day or observance and mostly in the more rural districts of the country. The parts of the sheep are divided in customary ways. The guest receives one of the choicest cuts, usually an eyeball, the brain, or meat from the right cheek. It is almost impossible to refuse such an act of generosity; seasoned travelers say that it is important to accept the offer and do your best to ingest whatever part is served. If you do have to refuse anything at any time, it is best to place your left hand over your heart as a sign of sincerity. The meal usually ends with tea and a prayer.

Another potential source of embarrassment can be the guest realizing that the hosts are providing more than they can afford. Veteran travelers say there is little to be done, except to refuse individual items whenever possible, using an excuse such as feeling ill. Sometimes a guest can give a gift of money to the eldest child, saying that it is for their education.

SHORPA (SPICED LAMB STEW)

This thick lamb-and-vegetable stew is a common hearty winter meal, and the colorful diced vegetables make it an attractive one. This recipe serves eight.

$^1/_4$ cup ($^3/_4$ kg) olive oil

$1^1/_2$ pounds ($^3/_4$ kg) stewing lamb in 1-inch (2-cm) chunks

1 medium onion, chopped

10 cups beef stock

1 large turnip, chopped into $^1/_2$-inch ($1^1/_4$-cm) pieces

1 large zucchini, chopped into $^1/_2$-inch ($1^1/_4$-cm) pieces

2 carrots, cut into $^1/_2$-inch ($1^1/_4$-cm) pieces

2 green peppers, seeded and cut into strips

$1^1/_2$ pounds ($^3/_4$ kg) tomatoes, chopped

$1^1/_2$ teaspoons cumin

$^1/_2$ teaspoon hot-pepper flakes

1 teaspoon ground coriander

1-pound ($^3/_4$-kg) can chickpeas (garbanzos), drained

salt to taste

3 tablespoons white vinegar

$^1/_2$ cup chopped cilantro

Heat the oil in a large Dutch oven, and brown the meat over high heat for about 5 minutes, stirring occasionally. Stir in the onion and cook for another 5 minutes, or until it is soft. Spoon off as much fat as possible, pour in the beef stock, and bring to a boil. Reduce the heat, cover, and simmer for about $1^1/_2$ hours. Refrigerate the soup, overnight if possible. This makes it easy to spoon off the fat gathered on the surface. About an hour before serving, skim the fat off the stew, then bring the liquid to a boil over medium heat. Add the chopped turnip, zucchini, carrots, peppers, tomatoes, then the cumin, hot-pepper flakes, coriander, and chickpeas. Cook, covered, for 30 minutes over medium heat. Add salt to taste, then stir in the vinegar. Cover and let stand for 15 to 20 minutes. Serve in soup bowls. Garnish each with the chopped cilantro.

NAN (FLAT BREAD WITH ONIONS)

Nan is the most common bread throughout central Asia. It can be made plain or with onions.

6 tablespoons butter
1^1/$_2$ cups chopped onions
^{3}/$_4$ cup lukewarm water
1 teaspoon salt
3 cups all-purpose flour

In a heavy 10-inch (25-cm) frying pan, melt 1 tablespoon of the butter over high heat. Add the onions, turn the heat to low, and cook for 3 to 5 minutes, stirring occasionally, until the onions are soft but not brown. Transfer the onions to a mixing bowl with a spoon and let them cool at room temperature. Melt the rest of the butter in the skillet, then pour it into a large mixing bowl. Add the lukewarm water and use a large mixing spoon to stir in the onions, salt, and 2^1/$_2$ cups of the flour, a little at a time. If necessary, beat in some or all of the remaining ^{1}/$_2$ cup of flour to make a dough that does not stick to your fingers. Form the dough into a large ball, then divide it into 16 pieces. Form each of the pieces into a ball 1^1/$_2$ to 2 inches (4 to 5 cm) in diameter. With a rolling pin, roll out each of the balls into a circle about 8 inches (20 cm) in diameter. Set the circles aside. Clean the frying pan and return it, ungreased, to the burner over high heat. When it is hot enough that a drop of water bounces in the pan, place one of the dough circles in the center. Brown for 3 to 4 minutes on each side, turning it with a spatula. Do not worry if the nan does not brown evenly. Place each cooked piece on a rack. Serve the bread in a basket. If any piece becomes limp or soggy after a day or two, bake on a cookie sheet at 250°F (120°C) for 10 to 15 minutes.

KYRGYZ *PILOV* (RICE PILAF WITH LAMB AND VEGETABLES)

This recipe serves six.

¹/₄ cup vegetable oil
1 pound (¹/₂ kg) shoulder of lamb, cut into 1-inch (1¹/₃-cm) cubes
3 large carrots, cut into strips about 2 inches (5 cm) long and ¼ inch (¹/₂ cm) wide
2 large onions, cut into strips like the carrots
3 cups unconverted long-grain white rice
2 teaspoons salt
¹/₂ teaspoon black pepper
6 cups cold water

In a 10- to 12-inch (25- to 28-cm) frying pan, heat the oil until it just begins to smoke a little, then add the lamb cubes and fry for 6 to 8 minutes, turning them constantly with a large spoon or spatula until lightly browned on all sides. Use a slotted spoon to transfer the cubes to a 4-quart (4-liter) casserole. Add the carrots and 3 cups of the onion strips to the oil and lamb fat still in the frying pan. Cook the vegetables over medium heat until soft, stirring frequently; then stir in the rice. Lower the heat and cook for about 2 minutes, stirring constantly, until the rice is thoroughly coated with oil. Transfer the contents of the pan to the casserole, and sprinkle with salt and pepper. Stir lightly to blend the ingredients. Pour in the water and bring to a boil over high heat. Reduce the heat to low, cover, and simmer for 20 minutes or until the rice is tender. Add more salt or pepper if necessary. Serve the pilov on a platter and spread the remaining raw onion strips over the top. Serve right away, with nan if desired.

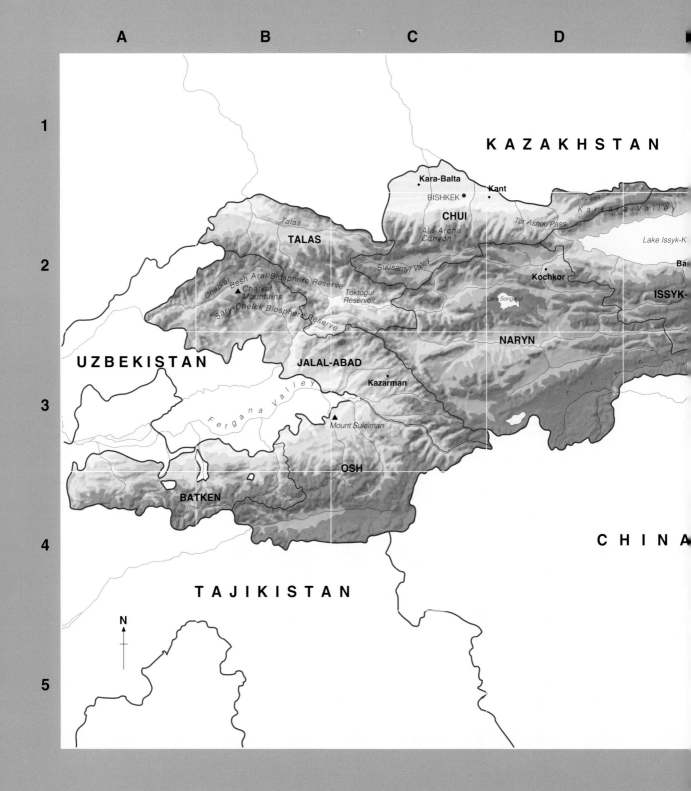

F

Khan Tengri
(22,998 ft / 7,010 m)

M u z t a g

Jengish Chokusu
(24,407 ft / 7,439 m)

Lake
Merzbacher

Inylchek glacier

─── International boundary
─── Regional boundary
● Capital city
• Major town
▲ Mountain peak

Feet	Meters
16,500	5,000
9,900	3,000
6,600	2,000
3,300	1,000
1,650	500

MAP OF KYRGYZSTAN

ECONOMIC KYRGYZSTAN

Natural Resources

 Coal

 Fish

 Gold

 Hydroelectric Power

Walnuts

Manufacturing

 Food Products

 Machinery and Instruments

Services

 Airport

 Tourism

Agriculture

 Cotton

 Grain

 Horticulture

 Livestock

 Racehorses

 Tobacco

 Vineyards

ABOUT THE ECONOMY

GROSS DOMESTIC PRODUCT (GDP)
US$8.5 billion (2004 estimate)

GDP GROWTH RATE
6 percent (2004 estimate)

GDP BY SECTOR
Agriculture 38.5 percent, industry 22.8 percent, services 38.7 percent

INFLATION RATE
3.2 percent (2004 estimate)

PER CAPITA INCOME
US$1,700

WORKFORCE
2.7 million (2000)

UNEMPLOYMENT RATE
18 percent (2004 estimate)

POPULATION BELOW POVERTY LINE
40 percent (2004 estimate)

CURRENCY
1 Kyrgyzstan som (KGS) = 100 tyin
USD 1 = KGS 40.9 (August 2005)
Notes: 1, 5, 10, 20, 50, 100, 200, 500, 1,000 som
coins: 1, 10, 50 tyin

LAND AREA
76,641 square miles (198,500 square km)

LAND USE
Arable land 7.3 percent
Irrigated land 5.5 percent

AGRICULTURAL PRODUCTS
Tobacco, cotton, potatoes, vegetables, fruit, grain, livestock

NATURAL RESOURCES
Gold, minerals

INDUSTRIES
Small machinery, textiles, food processing, community-based tourism

IMPORTS
US$775.1 million (2004 estimate)
Motor vehicles, appliances, electronics, clothing, food products, natural gas

EXPORTS
US$646.7 million (2004 estimate)
Wool, meat, cotton, tobacco, hydroelectric power, gold, silicon

MAJOR TRADE PARTNERS
Kazakhstan, Russia, Uzbekistan, China, Germany, Switzerland, the United States

CULTURAL KYRGYZSTAN

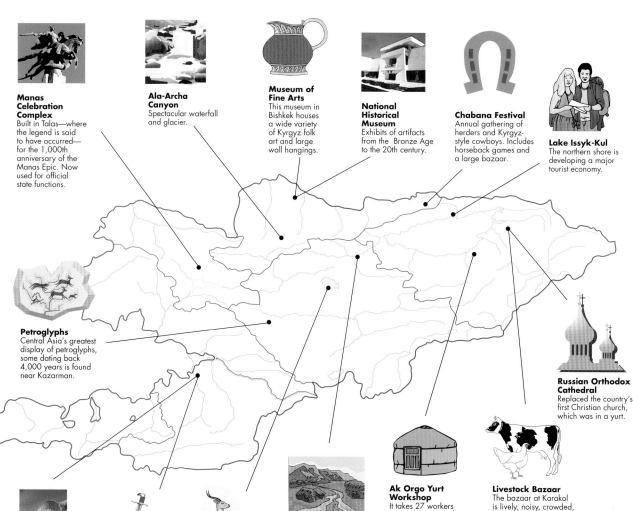

Manas Celebration Complex
Built in Talas—where the legend is said to have occurred—for the 1,000th anniversary of the Manas Epic. Now used for official state functions.

Ala-Archa Canyon
Spectacular waterfall and glacier.

Museum of Fine Arts
This museum in Bishkek houses a wide variety of Kyrgyz folk art and large wall hangings.

National Historical Museum
Exhibits of artifacts from the Bronze Age to the 20th century.

Chabana Festival
Annual gathering of herders and Kyrgyz-style cowboys. Includes horseback games and a large bazaar.

Lake Issyk-Kul
The northern shore is developing a major tourist economy.

Petroglyphs
Central Asia's greatest display of petroglyphs, some dating back 4,000 years is found near Kazarman.

Russian Orthodox Cathedral
Replaced the country's first Christian church, which was in a yurt.

Ak Orgo Yurt Workshop
It takes 27 workers two months to build one yurt. Price: $4,000.

Livestock Bazaar
The bazaar at Karakol is lively, noisy, crowded, and exciting.

Sarala-Saz
High mountain pasture (*jailoo*) where visitors take horseback treks through beautiful country. Horseback games are played each August.

Mount Suleiman
Above the city of Osh, this large jagged rock is a place of pilgrimage for Muslims, who believe the Prophet Muhammad once prayed there.

Silk Road Museum
Preserves weapons and other relics dating back 2,000 years.

Lake Song Kul
Tourist yurt camps are located in the Song Kul zoological reserve, where rare animals and birds are protected.

ABOUT
THE CULTURE

OFFICIAL NAME
Kyrgyz Republic

CAPITAL
Bishkek

OTHER MAJOR CITIES
Jalal-Abad, Karakol, Naryn, Osh

FLAG
A red background with a yellow sun in the center, upon which is a yellow *tunduk* (the framework surrounding the smoke hole at the apex of a yurt) symbolizing hospitality, national identity, and nomadic life.

POPULATION
5,081,429

POPULATION DENSITY
69 people per square mile

ETHNIC GROUPS
Kyrgyzs, Russians, Uzbeks, Ukrainians, Germans, Uighurs, Tatars, Kazakhs, Turks, Dungans, Koreans

LIFE EXPECTANCY
Men 63.8 years
Women 72.1 years

RELIGIONS
Islam, Russian Orthodox Christianity

OFFICIAL LANGUAGES
Kyrgyz and Russian

LITERACY RATE
97 percent (1993); it has declined since.

TIME
Greenwich Mean Time plus 5 hours
(GMT + 0500)

IMPORTANT ANNIVERSARY
Independence Day (August 31)

FAMOUS WRITERS
Chinghiz Aitmatov, Tolegen Kasymbekov, Suyunbai Eraliev, Alykul Osmonov

FAMOUS ARTISTS
Gaspar Aitiev (painter and sculptor), Olga Manuilova (sculptor), Jumabai Umetov (carpet weaver)

FAMOUS PERFORMERS
Toktogul (*akyn*), Muratali Kurenkeyev (musical instrumentalist), Kaiyrgul Sartbaeva (opera singer)

NATIONAL FOLKLORE
Manas Epic

TIME LINE

IN KYRGYZSTAN	IN THE WORLD
800–200 B.C. Scythians move into central Asia. First of the great nomadic empires.	**753 B.C.** Rome is founded.
200 B.C.– A.D. 400 Kushan empire of Iranian-speaking people absorbs the Scythians.	**116–17 B.C.** The Roman empire reaches its greatest extent, under Emperor Trajan (98–17).
100 B.C. The Silk Road is formed, opening trade between China and the West.	
A.D. 400–1200 Huns establish empires, followed by various Turkic tribes.	**A.D. 600** Height of Mayan civilization
750–800 Islam moves into central Asia.	
751 Central Asians defeat Chinese at Talas River.	
950–1000 Karakhanids, a Turkic people who had converted to Islam, establish an empire. Kyrgyzs migrate into the region.	**1000** The Chinese perfect gunpowder and begin to use it in warfare.
1200–1350 Genghis Khan establishes a huge Asian empire; his sons take over after his death in 1227.	
Late 1300s–1450 Timur the Lame (Tamerlane) establishes an empire.	**1530** Beginning of trans-Atlantic slave trade organized by the Portuguese in Africa.
	1558–1603 Reign of Elizabeth I of England
	1620 Pilgrims sail the *Mayflower* to America.
1685–1758 Ruthless Mongol Oyrats rule present-day Kyrgyzstan.	
1758–1862 Various khans rule parts of Kyrgyzstan. Russians seize Pishpek Fort (modern Bishkek); Russia rules most of Kyrgyzstan.	**1776** U.S. Declaration of Independence
	1789–99 The French Revolution

IN KYRGYZSTAN	IN THE WORLD
	1861 The U.S. Civil War begins.
	1869 The Suez Canal is opened.
1916–24 Kyrgyzstan is part of the Soviet Union.	**1914** World War I begins.
1928–32 Kyrgyzs are forced to give up nomadic ways and move onto collective farms.	
1930s Joseph Stalin's purges remove those he distrusts.	
1939–45 Soviet factories are moved from the western Soviet Union to Kyrgyzstan.	**1939** World War II begins.
	1945 The United States drops atomic bombs on Hiroshima and Nagasaki.
	1949 The North Atlantic Treaty Organization (NATO) is formed.
1950–80 Revival of Kyrgyz culture and Islamic practices	**1957** The Russians launch Sputnik.
	1966–69 The Chinese Cultural Revolution
	1986 Nuclear power disaster at Chernobyl in Ukraine
1991 Askar Akaev becomes president; Kyrgyzstan declares independence.	**1991** Break-up of the Soviet Union
	1997 Hong Kong is returned to China.
	2001 Terrorists crash planes in New York, Washington, D.C., and Pennsylvania.
	2003 War in Iraq
2005 Askar Akaev is forced from office.	

GLOSSARY

akim
The head man, or chief, of a tribe.

ak kalpak
A white felt cap with embroidery and a tassel; the standard headgear for Kyrgyz men.

akyn
A traditional songwriter and performer.

chaykana
A Kyrgyz teahouse.

ecosystem
An natural environment formed by the unique interaction between the plants and animals that live within it.

equestrian
Relating to horseback riding.

fundamentalism
Belief in an extreme form of a religion.

jailoo
High summer pasture.

kok boru
A game played on horseback, with a headless goat carcass as the object to be carried into a circle.

komuz
A three-stringed instrument played by plucking.

koumiss
A beverage made from fermented mare's milk.

mal bazari
The popular Sunday bazaar for buying and selling livestock.

manaschi
An *akyn* who has special skills in narrating the Manas Epic.

Nooruz
One of Kyrgyzstan's most popular festivals; also known as "New Day".

oblast
An administrative province of Kyrgyzstan.

rayon
A regional district within an *oblast*.

secular
Not relating or concerned with religion.

shyrdak
A handmade felt carpet that is Kyrgyzstan's best-known craft.

taboo
Something that is improper or unacceptable.

tunduk
The circular frame of wooden spokes that forms the apex of a yurt; also the central symbol on the national flag.

yurt
The portable tentlike dwelling of nomadic central Asians; still used in modern Kyrgyzstan.

FURTHER INFORMATION

BOOKS

Abazov, Rafis. *Historical Dictionary of Kyrgyzstan*. London: Scarecrow Press, 2004.

Aitmatov, Chinghis. *Tales of the Mountains and Steppes*. Moscow: Progress Publishers, 1969.

———. *The Day That Lasts More Than A Hundred Years*. Bloomington: Indiana University Press, 1988.

Asankanov, A., and N. Bekmuhamedova. *Akyns and Manaschis—Creators and Keepers of the Kyrgyz People's Spiritual Culture*. New York: United Nations Development Program, 1999.

Boulnois, Luce, and Bradley Mayhew. *Silk Road: Monks, Warriors and Merchants of the Silk Road*. Hong Kong: Odyssey Books, 2004.

Glenn, John. *The Soviet Legacy in Central Asia*. New York: Macmillan Press, Ltd., 1999.

Krippes, Karl A. *Kyrgyz-English/English-Kyrgyz Concise Dictionary*. New York: Hippocrene Books, 1998.

Maillart, Ella. *Turkestan Solo*. New York: G.P. Putnam's Sons, 1935.

Rashid, Ahmed. *The Resurgence of Central Asia*. Karachi: Oxford University Press, 1994.

Stewart, Rowan, Susie Weldon, Ceri Fairclough, and Paul Harris. *Kyrgyz Republic: Kyrgyzstan, the Heartland of Central Asia*. Hong Kong: Odyssey Books, 2004.

Thubron, Colin. *The Lost Heart of Central Asia*. New York: Heinneman, 1994.

Vitkovich, Victor. *Kirghizia Today*. Moscow: Foreign Languages Publishing House, no date.

WEB SITES

Central Intelligence Agency World Factbook (select Kyrgyzstan from country list). www.cia.gov/cia/publications/factbook

Kyrgyz Embassy, London. www.kyrgyz-embassy.org.uk

Kyrgyz handicrafts. www.kyrgyzstyle.kg/production

Video clips on Kyrgyz rural life, flora and fauna, and mountainous landscapes. http://bishkek.regency.hyatt.com/bishk/location_05.html

VIDEOS

Beshkempir (The Adopted Son). Directed by Aktan Abdykalykov. Fox Lober, 2004.

Bride Kidnapping in Kyrgyzstan. Directed by Petr Lom. Icarus Films, 2005.

Central Asia (Kyrgyzstan and Uzbekistan). Lonely Planet, 1997.

Kyrgyzstan, the Spirit of Central Asia. Touch-Ross Management Consultants, 1995.

Maimyl (The Chimp). Directed by Aktan Abdykalykov. Haut & Court, 2001.

Saratan. Directed by Ernest Adbyshaparov, 2004.

The Snowstorm Station. Bakyt Karagulov, 1995.

Travel Documentary on Kyrgyzstan and Uzbekistan. Pilot Film & TV Productions, 1995.

BIBLIOGRAPHY

Links to sites on Kyrgyzstan. www.kyrgyzstan.fantasticasia.net
Mayhew, Bradley, Paul Clammer, and Michael Kohn. *Central Asia*. Victoria: Lonely Planet, 2004.
Stewart, Rowan. *Kyrgyz Republic*. New York: W.W. Norton & Co, 2004.

INDEX